Football Made Simple

Ann Waterhouse

FOOTBALL
Made Simple

An Entertaining Introduction to the Game
for Mums & Dads

Illustrations by Amanda Stiby Harris

Meyer & Meyer Sport

British Library Cataloguing in Publication Data
A catalogue record for this book is available from the British Library

Football Made Simple

Maidenhead: Meyer & Meyer Sport (UK) Ltd., 2015
ISBN 978-1-78255-052-5

Previously published as *Sue Porter's Guide to Football* in 2014 by Ann M Waterhouse Ltd.

© 2015 by Meyer & Meyer Sport (UK) Ltd.
Aachen, Auckland, Beirut, Cairo, Cape Town, Dubai, Hägendorf, Hong Kong, Indianapolis, Manila, New Delhi, Singapore, Sydney, Teheran, Vienna

 Member of the World Sport Publishers' Association (WSPA)

Total production by: Print Consult GmbH, Germany, Munich
ISBN 978-1-78255-052-5
E-Mail: info@m-m-sports.com
www.m-m-sports.com

Dedication

This book is dedicated to that hardy band of supporters who stand by the sides of pitches across the country in pouring rain, howling wind and whatever else the British weather can throw at them, watching groups of kids kicking a large, round and very muddy ball up and down a field, occasionally interrupted by someone with a whistle who stops the game, only to start it again shortly afterwards.

Contents

Acknowledgements

The author would like to acknowledge the assistance she has received from friends and family, especially her husband David, sons Gareth and Alan and good friends who have ensured the accuracy of the text. I would especially like to thank John Davies, whose wisdom and extensive knowledge of the world's favourite team sport has been invaluable.

And last, but not least, Amanda Stiby Harris for her imaginative, amusing and illuminating illustrations. The books would be very different without her input, and the author is extremely grateful for her inspiration and talent.

I've been so lucky to have Amanda working with me on this series of books. If you're interested, her wonderful illustrations are available for sale in colour direct from Amanda. See her website for more information about her work:

» stibyharris.com

Introduction

This is the second book in our series of guides for supporters who are coming along to watch team games being played by their children, partners or grandchildren.

If you've picked up or been given this guide, we hope it's because you're interested in the game of football and want to learn more about it. We can't *guarantee* you'll enjoy watching the game more after reading our guide, but we're certain you'll be able to understand much more about what's going on, why the game's been halted by the *officials* and what may happen next, and who knows, maybe you will enjoy going along to matches more, too.

As with all sports, the more you understand the game, the more fun it is to watch. Knowing all the rules would be a step too far, but learning a little about the names of the playing positions, their roles on the pitch and some of the most important Laws of the game, will certainly help you enjoy those cold days sitting or standing by the sidelines.

In common with our other books in this series, we have highlighted familiar or well-used terms in *italics*, and quick explanations of these terms can be found in the glossary at the back of the book.

Whatever the reason for you reading this introduction, we hope you'll want to read on. We can guarantee some interesting facts, some useful guidance and definitely some humour about this highly popular game that inspires more passion from its followers than almost any other sport on the planet.

What is football?

'Football's football, if it weren't it wouldn't be the game that it is.'

(Garth Crooks)

Football is just simply the most popular *ball* sport in the world. Because all that is needed to play is an area of open space and a ball, much of the world's soccer is played informally on patches of ground without any marking or real *goals*, and in many places it is played barefoot, using rolled-up rags or newspapers as the ball. A major reason for football's vast popularity is its accessibility and adaptability.

The statistics are truly staggering: *FIFA* (Fédération Internationale de Football Association), the governing body of the game since 1904, estimates, through a 'Big Count' exercise, all those involved in football on a regular basis. The most recent took place in 2006, so even these figures are probably below current levels. Back in 2006, approximately 270 million people were involved in the game, 265 million players and 5 million officials. Just to put this into context, if footballers were a nation state, it would be the fourth most populous in the world. There are currently 29 million women and girls playing the game worldwide, and that number is increasing even more rapidly than the men's game.

The worldwide television audience for the 2014 World Cup final game was estimated by FIFA at 2.6 billion for those watching just a few minutes. The cumulative audience of all matches was estimated to be 26.29 billion with an estimated 715.1 million people watching the final in full. This means a ninth of the planet was watching.

This makes the World Cup Final game the most-watched single televised event, and it's a pretty good bet that at least one member of your close family watched this game. We know the total global audience for the Olympics is bigger, but that is spread over multiple sports and many days. The detailed review of the 2014 competition has not yet been published, but a single game (Brazil vs Croatia – the opening match) broke all records with just the Brazil-based audience totalling 42.9 million.

FIFA maintains an informative website, www.fifa.com, that provides so much detail it would take several weeks to read everything on the site, but if there are any statistics you'd like to check, that's the place to look first. Every nation has its own local organisation, the Football Association (FA) in England being the longest standing of these. They also have their own websites; for example, the FA one is www.thefa.com. You will find a list of the major websites in our web links pages at the back of this book and on our website:

>> www.sueportersguide.com.

Top Flight
International
football

Elite club football

Professional club football

Semi-professional football

Organised amateur football – teams

Unorganised amateur football – teams

Grassroots
Organised football – kids and others on a pitch

Unorganised football – kids in the park/street

Couch potatoes or fans – well, someone's got to watch

It is estimated that over 3.5 billion people in the world take an interest in the game, either playing or watching on a regular basis, but this figure is difficult to prove.

The hierarchy of football from grassroots to top flight teams is an extremely wide range. Here's our diagrammatic explanation:

In the next chapter, we'll explain a little about the game's formation and its development from ancient roots.

A brief football history

Football or soccer ... what's the difference?

Confusing, isn't it? There are many games around the world based on the same basic premise of kicking or heading a ball into a zone to score a goal, but the most popular of these sports worldwide is association football, more commonly known simply as football, or *soccer* – which is a slang term based on the contraction of the full name. Unqualified, the word, football, applies to whichever form of football is the most popular in that particular part of the world, and that includes American football, Aussie rules and Gaelic football.

There are also the variations which you may know as rugby (the rugby code is subdivided into Union and League), and you can find out more about Rugby Union in our companion book, *Rugby Made Simple*.

All these variations are known as *codes*, but that's nothing to do with how difficult they are to decipher, we promise. In terms of playing rules, rugby and football only split codes in 1863. Since it's the term that's accepted across the world, we will mainly refer to soccer as football throughout this book.

Media coverage

The game has been covered in the media for well over a century now, initially in newspapers, but with the advent of radio and television the descriptions of the game have been revolutionised. Legions of clichés have developed over the years as a result. Indeed it would be impossible for us to describe the game without using at least some of them. So we've included a few in our text which might be familiar – even to those of you who haven't already caught the football bug. We've also included some rich pickings culled from the commentators' bottomless pit of mixed metaphors, without which we would all be much the poorer.

The following diagram reflects some of the more imaginative commentary descriptions rather well; all the terms used in the diagram are also included in our glossary.

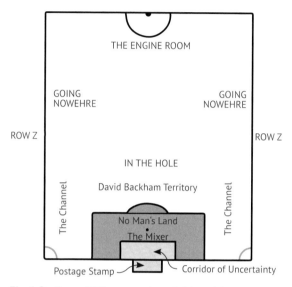

Fig. 1 Radio and TV commentary field positions

Row Z is, of course, right at the back of the stand, but to save space we've just indicated the seating area at the side of the pitch in our diagram.

You will hear commentators talking about balls 'coming from the *engine room*', attackers '*going nowhere* with the ball', defenders 'slotting balls *in the hole*' or 'into *David Beckham territory*', and wings 'taking the ball *down the channel*'. They will talk about *midfielders* moving into *no man's land* before getting into *the mixer*, and passing the ball to the striker for him to land the ball *on a postage stamp* in the top or bottom corner of the net. Good midfielders also pass the ball and land it on a postage stamp if they are very accurate.

Also, balls are hit by defenders into row Z with massive clearance kicks, and players taking corner kicks launch the ball into the *corridor of uncertainty.* Football commentary can be good fun to listen to, if only to pick out the stock phrases the commentators use for every game. A great commentator, like the BBC's legendary John Motson, or our current favourite Jonathan Pearce, will bring a game to life for you on radio or TV.

'When you're down … the fickle finger of fate rarely smiles on you.'
(Jonathan Pearce)

'Not the first half you might have expected, even though the score might suggest that it was.'
(John Motson)

Women's football

Women's football has been around since the inception of the professional game in the late 19th century, and there is evidence of female involvement in all the forerunners of the game, as well as medieval football games. Although not as popular with spectators yet, women's industry teams were actually extremely popular during World War I in Europe, including the famous Dick Kerr's Ladies from Preston, who also played the first international game against a team from Paris. With the young men at the front, the ladies' teams provided entertainment for the masses through difficult times.

In the UK, the sport was almost halted in its tracks when the Football Association decided to ban women's football in 1921, as it was then deemed to be in bad taste. Victorian attitudes to women's roles still prevailed despite the Suffragette movement. Women's football was finally revived following the formation of the English Women's FA as late as 1969 and the eventual lifting of the ban on women players in 1971. On a global level the game also expanded, and, by 1992, Japan had become the home of the first semi-professional women's league (the L. League).

Today, there are major international competitions, most notably the FIFA Women's World Cup and the UEFA European Women's Championship. In the UK, there are currently over 251,000 women footballers regularly playing (at least once a month). This is a significant increase from the 11,200 registered in 1993, confirming both the popularity of women's football and the cross-gender appeal of the sport generally. This figure is, however, slightly lower than the peak achieved in 2007-08.

If during our explanations in this book we refer to he or him, please don't think the information precludes the girls and women in our readership. It is just that it is simpler to stick to a single sex for our explanations. Indeed we could use the current Laws of cricket as our guide. These now state: *The use, throughout the text, of pronouns indicating the male gender is purely for brevity. Except where specifically stated otherwise ... this book ... is to be read as applying to women and girls equally as to men and boys.* In other words, just because we don't say she or her doesn't mean that everything we say won't apply to the fairer sex, too.

'She was a born footballer, even when she was young.'
(Eurosport)

Football through history

Humanity has been kicking round objects for fun for as long as they've both been around. However, more formal, organised ball games are a mere 4,000 years old, dating back to the first manmade balls. Around the world there are variations in the roots of football. In 1500 BC, the first solid rubber balls were made in Mesoamerica, and in 1200 BC, there were *olemac* ball courts used for ball games in the same region.

The Chinese game *cuju* is probably the most ancient game that relates closely to modern football, and it was first played and formalised during the Han dynasty around 200 BC. In the 7th century AD there is evidence of the game of *kemari* being played in the court of Kyoto, Japan. This game became really popular between the 10th and 16th centuries.

By 800 AD, the first recognisable football games were being played in southern Britain, and there are reports of *la soule* being played in France and street football in London by the 1100s. The first rules for *calcio* in Italy were published in 1580, and the first attempts to formalise *sepan tawak* in Malaysia took place in the 1750s.

Football is currently known all over the world as the beautiful game, although that term originally applied to other games, too, including tennis in the 19th century. In the late 1950s, it was a BBC radio commentator, Stuart Hall, who brought it into mainstream use, and the phrase is now intrinsically linked to football, having been used by superstar footballer *Pelé* in his autobiography title.

Although early versions of the game were first recorded over 3,000 years ago, the earliest records of using a ball made of a covered, air-filled inner bag (usually a pig's bladder), which bounced like the modern-day football, date back to the Middle Ages.

Some think the Norman conquerors from France brought the game to Britain after 1066, but there are records of football-like games as early as the 8th century in England, so the English staunchly claim the game is theirs – ancient rivalries with the French certainly stretch to all parts of life.

These early games were wild affairs, considerably less structured than modern games, with hundreds of people taking part. The extent of the game's popularity and boisterous nature back then is amply demonstrated by the fact that there were more than 30 royal and local laws passed between 1314 and 1667 that attempted to ban football in England. However, by the end of the 14th century, the term, football, was well established, with Chaucer even referring to it in his Canterbury Tales.

Variations on these original and somewhat manic games are played in Britain to this day, including several which are played annually on Shrove Tuesday; these include games held at Ashbourne in Derbyshire, Atherstone in Warwickshire and one at Corfe Castle in Dorset. If you live near any of these locations, you will no doubt have heard all about them, but if not, why not make a trip one Shrove Tuesday to see them in action.

It was perhaps these mayhem-filled games that formed the basis of the fevered support associated with the game to this day. Football fans have a very distinct reputation for passion, and even anger, when it comes to supporting their favourite team. We'll address fan behaviour later, but for now let's just say here that it's a game that arouses great passion in its followers.

During the 18th and 19th centuries, the game developed in schools and universities across the UK, using a whole variety of rules. Finally, the first official Laws of football were laid down in 1863 by the newly-formed Football Association. And here they are:

Pitch: maximum dimensions of 200 x 100 yards (180 x 90 m); goalposts should be 8 yards (7.32 m) apart, with no tape or cross bar.

A coin toss determines ends; kick-off to be taken from centre mark.

Sides change ends after every goal.

Goal scored if the ball is kicked between the two posts (at whatever height). [The addition of the goal top bar later changed this of course.]

Throw-ins to be taken by the player who first touches the ball after it has gone out of play. From the restart, the ball is not in play until it has touched the ground. [This must have led to major altercations between players to be the first to touch the ball. It's probably best this has now changed to the ball going to the opposite side from the player who last touched the ball prior to it crossing the sideline.]

When a player kicks a ball, any member of his team who is in front of him is offside. [How we wish the offside law had stayed this simple, but then football as we know it with long passes just wouldn't exist.]

No running with the ball in the hands.

No hands to throw or pass the ball.

No tripping, hacking, or holding.

We were fascinated by the history of football, and there's lots more to share with you, so we have included more detail that may interest you later in the book. If you prefer to continue learning about football's history now, just go to A little bit more history on page 110.

The game of football, as simply as we can

'To be a great game, one of the teams has got to score first.'

(Mark Lawrenson)

Football is a team game played by two teams of 11 players – although just to confuse the beginner there are also variations designed for as few as five-a-side. This is the first of the contradictions which seem to form a major part of the game of football. Understanding this game is going to be fraught with contradictions, but we'll do our best to guide you through them all.

The game of Association Football is played on a rectangular field – ideally covered in grass or green artificial turf – with a goal placed in the middle of each short end of the field. The object of the game is to score goals by kicking (or heading) the ball into the opposition's goal.

Football is played at so many levels, varying from a few children playing on any surface they can find where they can kick a ball, with coats and jumpers for goalposts, to strictly-regulated professional football matches played in purpose-built stadiums, between teams of highly-trained and highly-paid professional players in front of huge crowds of 100,000 or more all round the world. Just take a look again at our hierarchy diagram on page 12 to see the enormous range.

Around the world, unofficial games of football can last anything from a few minutes to hours, if energies permit. Official matches last just 90 minutes (45 minutes *each way* – 45 minutes with players playing towards the goal at one end of the pitch and then 45 minutes attacking the opposite end of the pitch).

Another contradiction for you: In reality, games can last quite a bit longer than 90 minutes, so don't imagine you can plan a social engagement 90 minutes after the start of the match. This is because there's a break at half-time that can last up to 15 minutes, and whenever there's an abnormal break in play, the referee stops his watch to ensure the full 90 minutes are used up actually playing the game, not dealing with injuries or bad play. At professional games, the additional time created by adding up all of the *stoppages* is then added on at the end of each 45 minutes as counted down on the stadium clock. The fourth official will hold up a board showing how many minutes of *added time* will be played before the first or *second half* can end, but this is rarely more than four minutes, suggesting there is some leeway in when the watch is switched on and off.

Cliché of the moment: It's a game of two halves!

Handling the ball (or not, as the case may be)

The first and simplest modern law of football is that only one member of each team is allowed to touch the ball with their hands or arms while the ball is inside the playing area. These lucky players are the *goalkeepers* (otherwise known as goalies, or keepers), whose job is to protect the *penalty* and goal area and prevent goals from being scored. They do this by blocking the ball with any and every part of their body, using feet, head, legs, arms and hands in equal measure. To help the officials manage the game, all goalkeepers wear different coloured *strip* from their team-mates to distinguish the players who can handle the ball from those who can't.

Just to be difficult, however, if the ball goes off the pitch at the *sidelines*, teams can select a player to throw it back in. That player is allowed to pick up the ball and throw it back onto the pitch, ideally at the feet or head of another player from his team to ensure their attack continues.

However, the throw-in player must ensure his feet stay outside the field of play as he launches the ball over the sideline. The action of throwing the ball is also strictly governed by the Laws. This results in some amusing contortions as players grasp the ball in both hands and throw it from behind their heads, whilst avoiding crossing the sideline with their feet as laid down in the Laws. They are frequently seen teetering on the brink before releasing the ball. Some players can throw an amazing distance, making their throw-ins as valuable as a corner kick to their team.

Other than *throw-ins*, no *outfield* players are allowed to touch the ball with their hands or arms; they must just use their feet, torsos and heads to move the ball around the pitch. If they do handle the ball, and the referee believes the action was deliberate, he will blow his whistle and award a free kick to the opposition. It's interesting too that *passing* the ball, which in the early days of football, before the rugby code split, meant a hand-to-hand movement, has now become a description for moving the ball around with the feet, chest or head.

'The goals made such a difference to the way this game went.'

'You couldn't count the number of moves he made; I counted four and possibly five.'

(John Motson)

'It was a good match which could have gone either way and very nearly did.'

(Jim Sherwin)

Who wins and penalty shoot-outs

Results of football matches are pretty easy to understand: The team that scores the most goals always wins the match. If the score is tied at the end of the game, either a draw is declared, or the game can be extended into *extra time* (usually 15 minutes each way at senior level), or the teams move into a *penalty shoot-out*.

This only happens in important matches, such as cup competitions or international games, where it has been agreed the result will be finalised on the day or night by the use of a penalty shoot-out competition. The teams will then line up five players from each side to take turns to take a penalty *shot* or *spot kick* at the opposition goal.

If at the end of the five attempts the score remains even, the shoot-out will continue on a goal-for-goal or *sudden death* basis, with the teams taking shots alternately, the winner being the team that scores a goal that is unmatched by the other team. This can continue until every player in the team has taken a shot – including the goalies – after which players may take additional shots until a result is decided.

Sadly someone has to be the player that misses or whose shot gets saved, and these individuals are frequently vilified by so-called fans. All good supporters understand that scoring from the penalty spot is one of the most difficult things a player has to do. Those who miss deserve our sympathy, not our anger, but unfortunately this has not been the rule amongst many passionate football fans.

England players who have suffered after missing important penalties include Frank Lampard, Steven Gerrard and Jamie Carragher, who all missed during the 2006 World Cup competition. In the 1998 World Cup, Paul Ince and David Batty both missed, and in 1990, it was the turn of Stuart Pearce and Chris Waddell.

Young players taking penalties need nerves of steel. If your youngster gets this role in his or her team, you know they're very special players.

Where to play – the pitch

'It was a bit like a game of chess, they kicked the ball from one end to the other.'

(John Monie)

The dimensions of the pitch have changed several times since the 1800s. In 1882, the addition of touchlines and goal lines became compulsory. Since then the size of the pitch has shrunk, and gradually blank muddy fields have become well-defined and precisely-marked pitches.

Here's a breakdown of how they've altered over the years:

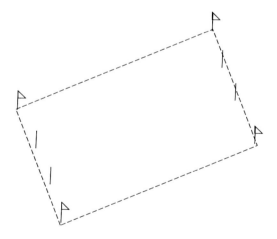

This is the first pitch based on the 1863 Laws. It has no pitch markings at all, even the line around the edge of our diagram wouldn't have been marked on the field. It just had corner flags and posts set 8 yards (7.3 m) apart. The field size was considerably bigger, too – up to 100 yards wide and 200 yards long (90 m x 183 m).

During 1872, a tape was hung between the goalposts at a height of 8 feet (2.4 m) above the ground. The tape was introduced after a goal was scored at Reigate, a town in Surrey, England that went between the posts, but it was 30 feet (10 m) in the air. The crossbar became a permanent feature in 1882, as did pitch markings around the boundary and a halfway line.

In 1887, the goalkeeper's area was marked with an optional 18-yard (16 m) line, right across the full width of the pitch. There is some confusion over the exact timing, but between 1887 and 1891 the centre circle and centre spot were introduced. The circle has a 10-yard (9 m) radius.

In 1891, goal nets were invented by John Alexander Brodie, and a line marking the pitch 12 yards (10.9 m) from the goal was introduced right across the pitch, and the pitch then looked closer to modern pitches in design. The area bounded by this line through to the goal line functioned as the newly-introduced penalty area, and a penalty could be taken anywhere along the line at this time. The following diagram shows the 12-yard line and the optional 18-yard line (16.5 m) (the dashed line in the figure).

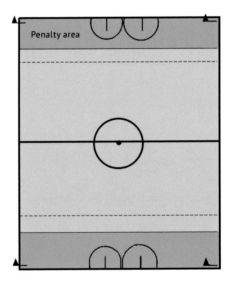

In 1902, the 18-yard (16 m) line was reduced in length, so it no longer reached from side to side of the pitch but become the boundary of the penalty area (or 18-yard box as it is known to this day), including the penalty spot. At the same time the 12-yard line was removed, and the goal area became known as the 6-yard box.

Finally, in 1937 the D, or arc, of the penalty area was added to ensure that all players, except the penalty taker and opposing goalkeeper, stand at least 10 yards (9.2 m) from the penalty spot when the ball is kicked. It's a mini exclusion zone.

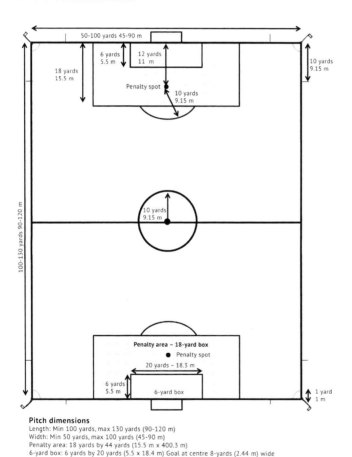

Pitch dimensions
Length: Min 100 yards, max 130 yards (90-120 m)
Width: Min 50 yards, max 100 yards (45-90 m)
Penalty area: 18 yards by 44 yards (15.5 m x 400.3 m)
6-yard box: 6 yards by 20 yards (5.5 x 18.4 m) Goal at centre 8-yards (2.44 m) wide
Corner marking 1-yard quadrant. Optional off-pitch marks show 10-yard distance from corner

Fig. 2: 1937 pitch diagram – the modern football pitch as laid down in the Laws.

The Laws of the Game

'A leader leads by example, whether he intends to or not.'
(Anon)

'Whether that was a penalty or not, the referee thought otherwise.'
(Brian Moore)

The modern Laws not only govern the layout of the pitch as we've already described, but also the type of ball to be used (currently this is a spherical ball of 28 in. [71 cm] circumference at senior level).

The Laws also detail unlawful actions and the penalties attached to them. Every referee and referee's assistant has to understand the Laws in detail in order to oversee a game.

For you to enjoy a game, there is no need for you to understand the Laws in full, but if you do want to check anything at any time, FIFA and the FA both have website versions available:

FIFA
>> www.fifa.com/aboutfifa/footballdevelopment/technicalsupport/ refereeing/laws-of-the-game/index.html

The FA
>> www.thefa.com/football-rules-governance/laws/football-11-11/law-1---the-field-of-play

Every football team is led by a captain who has only one official responsibility as mandated by the Laws of the Game: that is to be involved in the coin toss prior to kick-off or match-deciding *penalty kick* competitions. Of course, all captains should lead by example – another football cliché.

Football games and some football skills

'It seems that they're playing with one leg tied together.'

(Kenny Samson)

'My left foot is not one of my best.'

(Sammy McIlroy)

There are multiple variations of football being played around the world, including Futsal – otherwise known as *Futebol de Salão* – which is played across South America and the Middle East and Africa, based in sports halls marked for basketball. Now regulated by FIFA, it is a competitive game with completely separate laws. It uses a small heavy ball and is played at very high speeds.

In Britain it is played five-a-side, but in the USA and Spain, there are usually six players per side.

Beach soccer started out as an informal kick-about game but has now been developed for TV coverage. Each game is split into three 12-minute periods of play, and it is played in temporarily enclosed mini stadiums. Players wear neither shoes nor socks, pitch markings are minimal and there are no walls or sideboards allowed around the pitch.

Freestyle football is essentially juggling with the ball in as creative a way as possible. Any part of the body except the arms and hands can be used, just like traditional football, and at the highest level it is a cross between *keepy-uppy* (juggling to keep the ball in the air just using your feet), break-dancing and gymnastics with a few bits of martial arts thrown in. The World Freestyle Football Association was established in 2005 and laid down the basis on which players would be awarded points. There are so many ways for players to move the ball that listing them would fill three or four pages of our book, so we suggest you check out the latest information here:

» www.freestylefootball.org

In recent years *Paralympic football* has developed with adaptations for people with various disabilities. There are two main versions of Paralympic football, one for the visually impaired and another for those with disabilities linked to cerebral palsy. Those with sight impairments play a five-a-side game. Those with cerebral palsy, stroke sufferers or those with other kinds of brain injury play a seven-a-side variation.

There is also a deaf football league, and cup competitions take place under standard FIFA rules. Some deaf players go on to play in mainstream football to great success. Famous deaf players include Rodney Marsh of Queen's Park Rangers, Manchester City, Fulham and England who lost hearing in his left ear after a collision with John Sjoberg whilst scoring a winning goal against Leicester City in September 1963.

Finally, there are variations for those who have lost limbs, for whatever reason, and these are Wheelchair Football and Football for Amputees. In general, the latter is played in poorer countries where war injuries have caused the need for amputation. Wheelchair football is played in richer nations where wheelchairs are more readily available.

Street football has always been a city game, and the rules are far less stringent, with no offside rule and coats frequently acting as goalposts, or a goalmouth marked in chalk on a wall. Teams are often made up of differing numbers and with no officials the rules are also invented on the spot as the game progresses. Generations of players have honed their skills playing in these tight, crowded spaces.

We could give you details about all the variations, including Cubbies, 21, Four nets, Gol Para Mi, Munich, Points, Ten Shots and Shooties, but our role here is to explain regular Association Football to you. If these alternatives excite your interest, you can find lots of information available on the internet to complete your knowledge.

In Association Football, the Laws now dictate that within normal play, all the players are free to play the ball in any direction and move throughout the pitch, even the goalkeepers. However, the ball cannot be received by a player standing in an offside position without the team being penalised (more on that later – and we're ready to admit it's definitely the most complicated part of the game).

Of course goalies (as they are also known) rarely leave their *penalty areas*, otherwise the goal they are supposed to be defending would be left open to attack from the opposition. Occasionally, however, when important corner kicks are taken, their extra height (goalies are generally tall players) can help their team to score, and they will come up to the opposition penalty area for these *set piece plays*. If their team fails to score, they are then seen sprinting back up the pitch towards their own penalty area to prevent the opposition from scoring while the goal remains open to attack.

Football skills

'He's always been an excellent dribbler, both with and without the ball.'

(TalkSport)

Footballers move the ball across the ground by *dribbling* (i.e. running with the ball, controlling it with their feet), by *passing* the ball to a team mate (either along the ground or in the air) or by taking *shots* at the opposition's goal. They can also head the ball if it is high in the air, and it can be controlled easier by using the forehead.

All players can *chest* a ball if it arrives at that level of their body, as long as they avoid any contact with their arms or hands. Great passing kicks can sometimes bend in the air (thanks to the aerodynamic properties of the modern football). As a result, shots at goal frequently go in a banana-shaped trajectory, and the phrase 'bend it like Beckham', which later became a film title, refers to English player David Beckham's unerring ability to bend the ball in this way, especially around *walls* of players placed in front of goal, when taking direct free kicks.

Other methods of moving the ball include the *chip* and the *bicycle kick*. The chip is a flick of the ball with the foot just above the ground, sometimes to get it over an opponent's leg, or sometimes just to move it quickly to a team-mate rather than kicking it along the ground or passing it high in the air.

The bicycle kick, also called a *scissor kick* or overhead kick, is a physical move made by leaping up into the air and making a shearing movement with the legs to get one leg in front of the other whilst seemingly floating over the ground. This can either be done backwards or sideways and is spectacular to watch, especially when it sends the ball behind the player at pace and is done close to the net, resulting in a goal being scored. Players twist and turn whilst kicking the ball during this move and can completely bamboozle their opponents in the process.

Players regain control of the ball either by intercepting a pass or through tackling the opponent in possession of the ball. Physical contact between opponents is strictly restricted, however, and we'll explain the techniques of safe tackling later. Players can jostle each other and run shoulder to shoulder, but deliberate barging and shoving are both strictly prohibited, and *shoulder charging* is definitely not allowed.

If your child is interested in learning about football, you could check to see if there is a local coaching course near you. The FA has set up a joint training scheme with supermarket chain, Tesco, and there are over 100 full-time FA Tesco Skills Football coaches running after-school courses at more than 50 skills centres throughout England to help 5- to 11-year-olds improve their football skills.

In addition, during the school holidays, the FA Tesco Skills football coaches run free holiday football coaching sessions for children of all abilities to give them an introduction to the programme.

Finally, the programme works in over 1,000 primary schools every year, providing specialist football coaching for children and supporting teachers in their delivery of the sport.

You can find out the details here:

>> faskills.thefa.com

The Laws of the Game don't specify any particular player positions, apart from the goalkeeper, but a number of specialised roles have evolved over the years, and we will attempt to give you a guide to these in our next chapter.

Football is generally a free-flowing game. Play only stops when the ball leaves the field of play or when play is stopped by the referee for an infringement of the Laws. There are specific ways to restart the game after such stoppages, and we'll explain these, too.

The number of goals scored in a football match at professional level is rarely high. In fact, the average number of goals scored in the English Premier League in 2011-12 season was just 2.81 goals, and this was the highest number recorded since the inception of the Premier League in 1992. Subsequent seasons have failed to even reach this relatively low score.

In the English Premier League, the average number of goals scored, for all the 22 seasons, is just 2.63 goals per game, so the excitement apparent at football matches is not just about scoring goals; it's got a lot to do with the highs and lows of attack and defence and the thrill of the near miss as well. Passionate fans can engender a feeling of excitement at any game with their chanting and cheering, and we'll be explaining this later in the book.

Here's the average goal list from the Premier League's last 22 seasons – you can see how little it varies from year to year.

Year	Average goals	Year	Average goals
1992-93	2.65	1993-94	2.59
1994-95	2.59	1995-96	2.6
1996-97	2.55	1997-98	2.68
1998-99	2.52	1999-2000	2.79
2000-01	2.61	2001-02	2.63
2002-03	2.63	2003-04	2.66
2004-05	2.56	2005-06	2.48
2006-07	2.45	2007-08	2.64
2008-09	2.48	2009-10	2.77
2010-11	2.8	2011-12	2.81
2012-13	2.8	2013-14	2.77

At junior levels, goal tallies can be much higher, which makes watching a game more exciting, although if they are very high scoring, the games do have a tendency to be somewhat one-sided.

Matches at junior level where both sides can beat their opposing defenders to score lots of goals are rare, but in the very early days for every new team of players, and until young and inexperienced defenders really master the art of tackling, games can be very exciting for a new spectator.

The ball

'I felt a lump in my throat as the ball went in.'
(Terry Venables)

As we've already explained, once all the Laws of the Game were agreed, the properties of the official ball (in terms of size, weight and type) were also set down. Balls still seem to change on an almost annual basis, and balls developed for competitions like the World Cup occasionally cause controversy due to changes in their ability to swerve or bounce, which can bamboozle even the most skilful or highest-paid players in the world.

The oldest recorded leather football was only found in 1999, in the rafters above the bedroom of Mary Queen of Scots in Stirling Castle in Scotland. It has been dated back to over 450 years ago. It was made out of a leather-covered pig's bladder, and this was the type of ball used for many centuries before the advent of inflatable rubber inner linings and plastic-coated leather during the 20th Century.

Pigs' bladders were originally used uncovered, their unusual shape causing uncertain bounce and apparently adding to the excitement of the game, much as the oval balls used in rugby or American football do to this day. Henry VIII even had a pair of shoes especially for football listed in his Great Wardrobe in 1526. So football is truly a game for kings and commoners.

The whole essence of football is predicated on the ball and its properties. It has to be a particular type of ball, with the ability to fly through the air as directed by the player and to bounce predictably. It was probably the development of the bouncing ball and the sheer fun of kicking and manoeuvring it in a wide variety of ways which made football the world's most popular and successful game.

Eventually a rule created for the FA Challenge Cup in 1883 insisted that balls should have an average circumference of not less than 27 inches (68.5 cm) and not more than 28 inches (71 cm). A standard weight for a football was also set in 1889, at between 12 and 15 ounces (340-425 g). This was increased in 1937 to between 14 and 16 ounces (397-453 g).

Team positions

'Picking the team isn't difficult – it's who to leave out.' *(Kevin Keegan)*

Young players will take time to work out their best role on the pitch, but it's not unusual for sports teachers or coaches to choose two captains and let them 'choose' their preferred team during school or club practice sessions.

This results in a certain amount of stereotyping in the early days of a young footballer's career. The tall lads will get put in *defence*, the quick ones may get put out on the wings, and frequently the biggest kid in the class will end up in goal – not generally the most sensible place for him or her, but captains will soon work out that they don't actually move fast enough to chase the ball as it thunders towards the goal, and you can be certain they'll put them in a different position next time around.

If your kid comes home complaining he or she is the last one to get picked for the team, you have at least a couple of options: help them to improve their skills by joining the local junior club, or find another sport where they can excel. Track and field athletics provide opportunities for bigger kids – let's face it, shot putters are rarely small individuals – and rugby football can always use a hunky kid in the scrum and will certainly ensure they get fitter.

As for the smaller slighter kids, their talents may well not lie in team sports, but bear in mind there are individual sports where they can shine, too, like long-distance running, tennis, badminton, squash, fencing, judo, karate or even triathlon.

Developing skills in other sports will improve their confidence and help them realise it doesn't really matter if they are the last to be picked for football.

Team captain

Wearing the captain's arm band is a responsible role that should be taken very seriously. If your child or partner has been appointed captain for the day, or even the entire football season, you can feel very proud of them. The best captains inspire their teams to play well, encourage the less able and praise all their players in equal measure to ensure team harmony.

Here's a tongue-in-cheek suggestion of what makes a perfect footballer based on some familiar commentary descriptions. You may have heard that a misfiring striker needs to watch his backside, for instance. Or that a hard defender doesn't have a malicious bone in his body (despite copious evidence to the contrary). Our new player will obviously need an educated left foot, a good eye for goal and an old head on young shoulders if he's going to be successful!

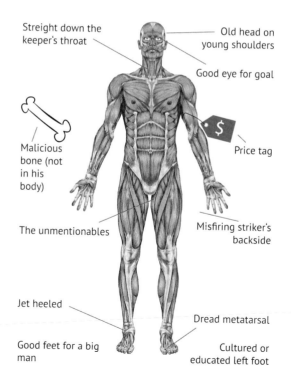

Streight down the keeper's throat

Old head on young shoulders

Good eye for goal

Malicious bone (not in his body)

Price tag

The unmentionables

Misfiring striker's backside

Jet heeled

Dread metatarsal

Good feet for a big man

Cultured or educated left foot

'We say educated left foot – of course there are many players with educated right foots.'

(Ron Jones)

The main outfield positions are

strikers or *forwards* whose main task is to score goals;

defenders and *sweepers*, who specialise in preventing their opposition from scoring; and

midfielders, who spend the match dashing from one end or one side to another, trying to stop the opposition scoring by taking the ball away from them, and then passing it on to their own forwards to allow them to score goals instead.

However, a player's main role doesn't stop him from taking on other roles during a match. Attackers are expected to drop back and defend, and defenders regularly score goals. The stature of defenders means they can be a potent attacking force at set piece plays, such as during corner kicks.

Famous footballers abound, so choosing just one name for each of these roles would be impossible, but just to help you recognise these roles, famous strikers have included Gary Lineker of England, Diego Maradona of Argentina, and of course the best known of all, Pelé from Brazil, who also played in an attacking midfield position during his long career.

Current attacking stars include: Lionel Messi and Luis Suarez of Barcelona and Argentina and Uruguay; Manchester United's Robin van Persie who also plays for The Netherlands national team, and Wayne Rooney of England.

Defenders and midfield players

Perhaps the most famous midfield footballer in the modern game is David Beckham. As famous for his football skills as for his celebrity lifestyle, marriage and charitable work, David is an icon of modern football. Other famous midfielders include Cristiano Ronaldo, the Portugal national team captain, currently with Real Madrid, and Cesc Fàbregas of Spain and Chelsea FC.

Famous defenders include Vincent Kompany of Manchester City and Belgium and Sergio Ramos of Spain and Real Madrid.

The best goalkeepers ever have included England's Gordon Banks, a legend from the 1960s, and Peter Schmeichel, Manchester United's and Denmark's long-serving keeper from the latter part of the 20th century. Currently, Germany and Bayern Munich's goalkeeper, Manuel Neuer, is world leading. Others in the top 20 include Tim Howard of Everton and the USA and Joe Hart of Manchester City and England.

If you want to discover who the main players in the world are, you can find many of them listed on websites such as:

>> www.worldsoccer.about.com
   or
>> https://www.easports.com/fifa/news/2014/fifa-15-player-ratings-top-20-goalkeepers

All the players – apart from the goalkeeper – are known as *outfield* players. Each of these outfield roles are further subdivided and named after the area of the pitch where they play. For instance, there are central defenders, left and right midfielders, left and right backs.

You're probably getting the idea; this isn't going to be simple!

As you've already learned, the 10 outfield players can be arranged on the pitch in any formation they choose. The number of players in each part of the pitch determines a team's playing style; using more forwards and fewer defenders creates a more aggressive and offensive game, and the reverse layout can result in a more deliberate, defensive team.

While players can spend most of the game in a specific position, there are few restrictions on player movement, so players are allowed to switch positions at any time. Indeed, some players are famous for roaming around the pitch in search of the ball and a chance to get involved in the game regardless of their nominated position.

This is usually discouraged at school level as it can lead to all 20 outfield players chasing the ball and to calls of 'don't muddle' from the coach!

Defining the team's formation and tactics is usually the prerogative of the team's coach at school and junior club level and in professional football it falls to the club's manager. Top-flight club management has changed in recent years with the addition of a director of football and a general manager to the standard managerial team.

It's not entirely clear what these new roles are within coaching the team. In truth, it seems they get involved very little in coaching matters; their role is more business managerial, allowing the manager to concentrate on training the team and preparing them for matches while the director of football or general manager liaises with the board and gets involved in marketing the club.

Directors of football are usually former players and managers, and this can lead to the kind of disputes with current managerial incumbents that have destabilised large clubs in England since the introduction of the role. However, there have been a few really successful occupants of this role, and Bobby Charlton at Manchester United is just one of them.

Individual player positions

'He's got a left foot, and left foots are like bricks of gold.'

(Jimmy Greaves)

If your child has just taken up football, you'll naturally want to know where they play so you can look out for them, but don't expect certainty on their pitch position right from the start.

Some children will star in a particular role early on, but most will develop over time. Who would have thought that 6-foot-6 (2 m) tall Peter Crouch would make an outstanding striker when he was a gangly teenager? Not many, I'm sure.

If your little footballer runs like a cheetah but is small, he will probably fit well into a football team on the wing. If he's sturdy and tall for his age, he'll probably make an excellent back (defender). But the joy of football is that players come in all shapes and sizes, and these days the only distinguishing factor is skill level, not size or shape. The best thing you can do is encourage your youngsters to hone their ball skills, and then they will be able to play almost anywhere on the pitch.

In terms of skill, all players will favour one foot over the other, but the very best footballers become equally proficient with both feet. The importance of having a 'good left foot' is obvious when you realize that crossing the ball from the left-hand side of the field into the penalty area is so much easier using that foot.

If you can encourage your young players to kick the ball equally well with both feet, they will become great assets to any team they may join.

Here's a list of possible positions that you might hear mentioned in radio or TV commentary or in family discussions. We should also mention that the terms used to describe players will vary depending on which generation is talking about them:

- Goalkeeper
- Right back
- Left back
- Centre back
- Full back
- Wing back

- ◦ Central defender
- ◦ Sweeper
- ◦ Right wing/Wide midfield
- ◦ Left wing/Wide midfield
- ◦ Centre half/Centre midfield
- ◦ Centre forward/Striker
  and finally ...
- ◦ Behind the striker (see our 4-4-1-1 formation diagram on page 65). This position is also known as *playing in the hole*. See our commentary diagram on page 15.

Summing this all up, you now know that a football team is made up of 11 players who can be assigned individual positions on the pitch. So let's give you some more detail on each individual role and what they do during a match.

The goalkeeper

'If you stand still, there's only one way to go and that's backwards.'

(Peter Shilton)

'Apart from picking a ball out of the net, he hasn't had to make a save.'

(Ron Atkinson)

Sadly, at junior level, it has been traditional for the fattest kid in the class, who naturally hates running up and down, to get to stand in goal and be humiliated by his fellow pupils as they run around him, scoring goals at will.

These days, tall kids also end up in goal – their height giving them the advantage in stopping the ball from entering the goal near the top of the frame. Sometimes there's a tubby and tall kid who's obviously destined for greater things ... and big hands are another major advantage for any goalie.

Of course, what you really need to be a great keeper is agility and bravery combined with intense concentration. If you play for a particularly good attacking team, it can get quite lonely between the sticks, but you need to remain alert for that crucial save, especially if you have not had much to do during the game until that point.

Goalkeepers are frequently blamed for a bad result, even when they are badly let down by their defensive line and the team's strikers fail miserably to score any goals. However, if they keep a *clean sheet*, and prevent the opposition from scoring any goals at all, then they become heroes. It's certainly a roller coaster life being a goalkeeper.

Goalies have had to significantly improve their foot skills in recent years since changes to the back pass laws mean they are no longer allowed to pick up a ball that is kicked directly towards them by one of their own team.

Defenders can head or chest a ball back to their keeper, but if they kick it towards him, he is obliged to kick it away, and he is definitely not allowed to touch it with his hands. If the goalie uses his hands and picks up the ball when he shouldn't, he will give away an indirect free kick which, with his proximity to the goal, may well result in the opposition scoring.

In the early days of this new rule, keepers brought up with the habit of always picking the ball up with their hands lacked the ball skills with their feet to cope and frequently scuffed the ball instead of clearing it cleanly under pressure, allowing poaching strikers to score at will. Over time, top-flight goalies have significantly improved their foot skills, so this rarely happens nowadays.

For a new young player, the most important aspect of being a keeper is having the best pair of gloves for the job and being willing to throw yourself around on the pitch whenever a ball comes within range. It would seem that bounce-ability is as important as football skills. See our guidance on choosing keeper's gloves in our kit section on page 91.

You can understand how being a goalkeeper is one of the glory and blame roles on the football pitch. If they save a goal from being scored, they're hailed as heroes; if they allow goals in, they can get the blame for the team losing the match.

Broad shoulders and a strong personality will certainly help goalkeepers from suffering too badly when their team-mates round on them after a particularly poor performance. Even if the whole team has performed badly, goalkeepers can still get the blame. It's all part of learning that life's not always fair – something team sports teach better than almost anything else in life.

Defenders: backs and sweepers

'It was a terrible challenge. He had his legs decapitated.'

(Colin Gibson)

'He went down like a sack of potatoes and then made a meal of it.'

(Trevor Brooking)

Generally known as the hard men of football, it's no surprise that famously rough defenders, such as Vinnie Jones, have ended up as Hollywood tough guys. There can be up to five defenders: a left back, up to three centre backs and a right back. Backs are usually the final line of defence before the goalkeeper. Their roles in preventing goals from being scored cannot be overemphasized; if they fail to tackle the attacking player and take the ball away, the opposition will nearly always score. These are the players standing in a row or arc in front of the goalie in our formation diagrams from page 62.

Football pundits say that good attacking football starts with a solid defence. For defensive players, there is no better feeling than making a timely sliding block or chasing after a striker and succeeding in taking the ball away from them. Whereas scoring is vital in football, most managers or coaches will be just as happy to see their players stopping goals from being scored.

Backs and goalies can both make long kicks to clear the ball away from their goal area, aiming it at the opposite end of the pitch. Sadly, at junior level, these *clearance kicks* are often inaccurate. They frequently fail to link up with their strikers, landing in front of their opposite numbers at the other end of the pitch, but they act as an effective defensive tactic in preventing goals from being scored, albeit temporarily.

If the backs succeed in preventing the opposition from reaching the goal and scoring, they will rapidly become the heroes of the team.

Alternatively, they can also be the ones who get the blame for letting the opposition score. Being the last defender between an attacker and the goal (we're obviously ignoring the goalie in this) is a pretty thankless task. If your small son or daughter is playing in one of these positions, just hope they have done loads of tackling practice and can become saints rather than sinners.

Good, safe tackling is a highly developed skill that takes years to learn, and defenders are really quite limited in how they are allowed to tackle their opponents. They can't tackle

◦ from behind,
◦ with their studs showing, or
◦ with their feet high above the ground.

This latter move is known as a high tackle and is immediately penalised by the referee, giving the opposition a free kick and often a yellow card to the defender. Sometimes, if the tackle is considered dangerous, it results in a straight red card for the offending tackler who then has to leave the pitch immediately and is not allowed to rejoin the game.

Other bad tackles include vicious *shoulder charges* (running shoulder to shoulder with your opponent is fine) and shoving an opponent off the ball. Sadly, the worst tackles imaginable can take place on the pitch if players think the referee is looking the other way and might miss these misdemeanours. They will soon learn this is pointless, however, as they rarely escape unpunished with the assistant referees also keeping an eye open for such bad behaviour. Intelligent players soon learn that *fair play* is the most sensible path to follow if they are to continue playing throughout a match without being sent off.

Good tackling is both a science and an art. Ideally your youngster will be encouraged to play the game in good spirit and will learn to tackle correctly. That way they will never need to resort to *foul* play.

Centre backs fill in the areas between the right and left backs and the midfield players, and they are used in the 4-4-2 formation (see page 63) as well as the 5-3-3 and other similar back-heavy formations. They need to be good tacklers and strong in the air. An ability to read the game and spot where likely dangers might emerge will be their greatest asset. They have to concentrate throughout the match and can't afford to relax for a single second. They even need to be aware that if their own keeper is clutching the ball, they should make themselves available for a pass.

The sweeper

The sweeper has absolutely nothing to do with brushing aside the opposition – or using a broom for that matter. This position is known in Italian as *libero*, or free, but it is only seen occasionally today.

The role of the sweeper is to act as an all-purpose defender, who responds to any breach of the defensive line. He acts as the final line of defence, apart from the goalie, and also initiates counterattacks by bringing the ball out of the penalty area, so he needs the skills of a midfielder – passing, close control and dribbling. Franz Beckenbauer – the famous

1974 German World Cup-winning captain – was widely credited as originating this role.

Full back/Wing back

In earlier times, the two wing backs were known as full backs, and together with one or two centre backs, they made up this main line of the defence. The back defensive line can include up to five players, but in the 4-4-2 formation they are now called central and wide defenders.

Although they sometimes have the same starting position as the traditional full back in the row of defenders in front of the keeper, wing backs are more willing to move forward to initiate and support attacks by their team (like the sweeper). They can do this by overlapping with the midfielders to add further width to an attack, but they still need good defensive skills. It's worth noting that some modern managers, including Fabio Capello and José Mourinho, prefer to use purely defensive full backs in these positions.

To be a useful wing back, you've got to be good at all parts of the game: fit, strong, good with both feet, a great tackler, an amazing passer and a fine crosser of the ball.

Good wing backs can be a real nightmare to defend against, as you're never quite sure where they'll turn up next, and with their amazing pace (they're usually the best sprinters on the park), they can escape a tackle or chase after the ball much easier than most of their opposition.

Midfielders

Midfielders are spread right across the middle area of the pitch. Situated in what is naturally the busiest area of the field, the central midfielder's task is to provide support to both defence and attack. Such is the complexity of this position that it has been split into categories that indicate the player's particular role, be it defensive or attacking. One of their main skills is *marking*. They pick a particular player from the opposition and track his every move – marking him – in order to prevent him from being too creative with the ball.

Defensive midfielder/Holding midfielder

This player will sit just behind the centre circle and is mainly expected to break down opposition attacks as well as help out the defence in general. Because he ends up in possession of the ball on a regular basis, he can also initiate attacks for his own team, so he is truly a multitalented player.

Playmaker

The playmaker stands in the same area of the pitch as the holding midfielder; by taking advantage of the latter's protection, the playmaker can influence his side's attacking game in a more concerted way. He takes advantage of the extra support he receives to send passes up to the attackers in his side and instigate quick offensive moves. Of course at junior level, the playmaker frequently starts attacks that his fellow players fail to understand, and it all ends with the opposition getting the ball back, but as the team get to know each other, playmakers can significantly influence the way a game proceeds.

Box-to-box midfielder

The all-rounders of the team, these players can play at either end of the field, and you may have seen or heard of Steven Gerrard (formerly of Liverpool and England) who played in this role. They're known as the *box–to-box* midfielders because they travel to and fro, up and down the full length of the pitch between the two penalty boxes.

They are sometimes described as the orchestra conductors, the engines of the team, the players that pull the strings from the middle. They certainly need loads of stamina as this position involves endless running around the pitch. Recent research has found players run 9.5 miles (15.3 km) in matches in the USA, and Wayne Rooney of England is renowned for running an average of over 7 miles (11 km) per match.

Players starting in this position also have superb football skills, and this position is a frequent inclusion in Premiership sides. If a school team uses a box-to-box midfielder, he will be a truly exceptional player.

These players will need to be strong tacklers in order to win the ball back for their team, and they must also have the skill to create opportunities for the strikers ahead of them. Sadly, a lot of their work goes completely unnoticed as they make forward runs to join their strikers. Just to complicate matters, they must also watch their opposite number and match his runs to assist in defence.

Attacking midfield or 'hole' player

The attacking midfielder occupies the space between the main midfield and the strikers, so he will be directly involved in the attack high up the field in the hole (also on our commentary position diagram on page 15). They frequently get to fill in as forwards as they are renowned for their goal-scoring abilities. Cristiano Ronaldo now plays in this role, which first emerged after the arrival of Pelé, who from attacking midfield scored an incredible 1,087 goals in 1,120 games for his Brazilian side, Santos. Of course, this was David Beckham's favourite position, too.

Forwards

'Oh he had an eternity to place that ball ... but he took too long over it.'

(Martin Tyler)

In the past, there were left and right wing forwards, inside right and left forwards, and centre forwards. The latter are now called the strikers and are usually the major goal scorers in any team.

In fact, if they're not scoring goals regularly in professional teams, they are unlikely to keep their place in the team for long.

Strikers

Possibly the easiest role on the pitch to explain, the striker's sole aim is simply to score goals. These players tend to stand just behind their opponents' penalty area and vary in number from one to three.

The striker and his close companions (depending on the team formation, of course) rarely leave the area just outside the penalty area of the goal they are attacking. Some strikers lack pace, but they make up for that in speed of thought and an ability to move away from their opposition markers to create goal-scoring chances.

It goes without saying that most of the top strikers in the world are selfish in front of goal, and their finishing skills are absolutely deadly.

If they touch the ball in the penalty area, they expect to score more often than not.

Very occasionally towards the end of a tight match, they will track back to help their team defend a lead, but their role is primarily an attacking one, and their location on the pitch amply demonstrates this. It's vital they are in a position to pick up a long pass from their defence and strike the ball at the opposition goal as quickly as possible.

They are praised and cursed in equal measure, depending on their rate of success. Strikers who fall out of the habit of scoring in every match can sometimes go for a long period before the muse returns to help them score freely again. During such periods, their 'supporters' have been known to be less than supportive. The FA's Respect programme hopes to change this, and certainly if you're coming along to football for the first time to watch your child play, it's good to remember that supporting your player through good and bad times is an important aspect of being a good spectator in the 21st century.

The playing styles of strikers vary, so here are a few of the variations.

Target man

These players stand inside the penalty area whenever possible to make themselves a focal point for attacks. They are opportunistic, often called poachers for this reason, and they are consummate *headers* of the ball. They rely completely on the provision of the ball from midfield or wing. If your young player is a little taller than average and learns to head the ball well early on, he would be perfect in this position. During his playing career, Alan Shearer was an outstanding target man, and TV presenter Gary Linker was a legendary poacher.

Withdrawn striker/Deep-lying forward/Number 10

A bit like the offside rule, trying to explain this role is not easy, even though some of the greatest footballers in history have taken it on. He's the chap standing behind the striker on our 4-4-1-1 diagram on page 65.

This player has equal goal-scoring and creative abilities. Originally made popular by Ferenc Puskás who played for the great Hungary side of the 1940s and 1950s, it became even more desirable when Diego Maradona of Argentina played here. In fact, his shirt number, 'Number 10', has become synonymous with the role ever since. Of course, as you would expect with a worldwide game, this position has different names in different parts of the world: Number 10 in South America and England, the *trequartista* (the three-quarter) in Italy and the nine and a half in France.

Withdrawn strikers will sometimes drop into the area between the opposition midfield and defence, giving themselves more time and space on the ball, and they are usually very difficult to mark as a result. They can be playing quite deep one minute and then burst forward to link up with their striker the next. Very comfortable on the ball, they generally have great vision and a very quick turn of pace. They create lots of chances for their team-mates and are also very capable of scoring.

Well that's it. Hopefully our explanations have helped to clarify what the different roles on the pitch are for. If you're still feeling unclear, why not look up the position that your young player tells you he is playing on the Internet, and we're certain you'll find more explanations than you can possibly imagine to help you understand what they should be doing during a game. We can certainly recommend the BBC Sport website as an excellent research tool.

Playing out of position

Much is made of how the 11 players spread themselves around the field, with the goalkeepers constrained by only being allowed to handle the ball inside the defined penalty area. As we explained earlier, if they handle the ball outside that zone, it will give the opposition a free kick.

As we've already explained, they do leave their area occasionally when their team is in urgent need of a goal, and they join their team-mates in the opposition penalty area, using their additional height to help with corner kicks and free kicks. Their addition to the attack can sometimes help their team outnumber and out-jump the opposition and can result in goals being scored.

All players can opt to move around the pitch, of course, and play the ball 'out of position', but defensive needs tend to constrain these moves, so most players stick to their assigned roles and locations on the pitch for the majority of a match.

Starting a game – the toss

If you're attending your first football game, you'll need to understand just a few more things. At the beginning of the game, both teams come out onto the pitch. The referee (one of three officials ensuring fair play during the game) will call over both team captains, and they will stand over the centre spot, while he tosses up a coin to decide which team will kick off and which direction the teams will play.

The captain winning *the toss* gets to choose which way his team will play, with the teams swapping ends for the second half of the match. The opposing team then kicks off. In the second half, the team that originally won the toss will kick off, having swapped ends with their opposition.

Choosing which end to attack is an important decision. If there is a slope in the pitch or a strong wind coming from one end of the pitch, the captain can choose to give his team this advantage in the first half,

hoping to score early and demoralise their opponents, or choose it for the second half when his team will be tiring and will enjoy the benefit of the wind on their backs or the downhill slope to the opposition goal.

If a professional team is playing at their home ground, their most fervent (and noisy) supporters will frequently be placed at one end of the stadium behind one of the goals, and, again, choosing when to take advantage of their support can be key to a good result.

Being team captain is an important position. Let's hope your captain always makes the right decision when choosing ends.

Team formations

Cliché of the moment: They're playing 4-4-2

The diagrams on the following pages show formations for football teams in match situations. At kick-off, all the players from a team must be standing in their own half (like the following diagram). We've removed the corner flags from all these diagrams to simplify them.

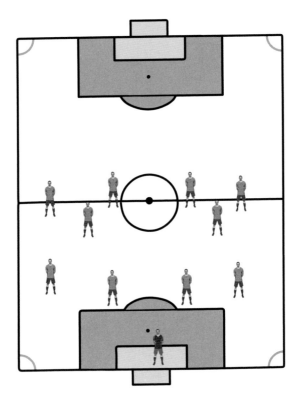

The most common pitch formation for a team is the well-known and much discussed 4-4-2 arrangement of players.

This means there will be four defenders standing in front of the goalkeeper, four midfielders standing in front of them and then two strikers up front, attacking the opposition goal. It's an adaptable system, which provides strength midfield and plenty of width to play across the pitch. Having two strikers means that each of the forwards has extra support when they receive the ball, rather than having to wait for midfield players to reach them.

The formation tends to free up the full backs (or wing backs) who stand at the sides of the defence and can end up with more time playing the ball than the midfielders, particularly if the opposition are using the same formation.

Other variations include 3-5-2 or 4-5-1; in fact anything you can imagine for 10 players spread around the pitch. Changes to these tried and tested formats in mainstream Premier League teams cause great consternation for fans. New managers trying new layouts are frequently criticised, especially if the new system fails to provide immediate success.

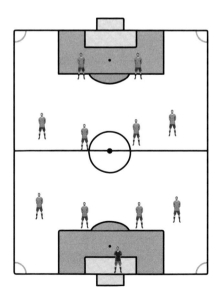

a. 4-4-2 formation

Here's the alternative 4-3-3 layout:

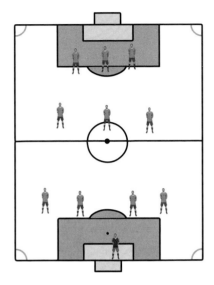

b. 4-3-3 layout

And the variable 3-5-2 or 5-3-2 option (we've marked the moving players who vary this formation):

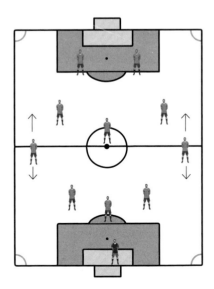

c. 3-5-2 or 5-3-2 option

Or a team could play 4-5-1:

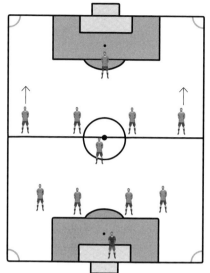

d. 4-5-1 formation

Or 4-4-1-1:

e. 4-4-1-1 formation

And finally here we have the rarely used 4-2-3-1 formation:

f. 4-2-3-1 formation

By now you'll be getting the idea that the players could actually stand almost anywhere on the pitch and a game of football would happen, and indeed that's how informal games work all around the world.

We also hope that you now understand that there are specific roles and responsibilities attached to each of the pitch positions. Players will train hard to master these during their football careers, and a spread of players across the pitch is vital for open, fast-moving football.

It's amazing how many different ways a team can line up at the start of a match, isn't it? Hopefully you're getting a feel for them all, but if nothing else, when someone mentions the ubiquitous 4-4-2 formation, now you'll know what they're talking about.

The officials, infringements and penalties

'There was no doubt about it, so the referee gave the defender the benefit of the doubt.'

(Dave Bassett)

'Sam Allardyce has backed the FA's decision to overturn the referee.'

(Alan Brazil)

A team of at least three officials look after every game of football. At senior level, there is also a fourth official whose role is to stay near the team benches to check substitutes prior to allowing them onto the pitch, and he informs the player being replaced that he is to leave the game. For televised matches, there is also a fifth member of the team based in the media room who can review TV footage to help referees make good decisions.

For junior club and school matches, there will generally be a referee on the pitch and a couple of assistant referees (officials who used to be called linesmen) standing on each *sideline*. At junior level, these assistants may well be members of the school team's substitutes' *bench* who are awaiting their turn on the pitch.

The assistant referees are only responsible for half of the pitch each, and because they are standing to one side of the pitch, action happening on the far side can be difficult for them to observe, so the referee's overall view of the game is vital. Between the three of them, they are responsible for ensuring the game is played fairly and for indicating when the ball goes off the side of the pitch (for a *throw-in*) or off the end of the pitch (for a *goal kick* or *corner kick*). They also indicate when a goal is scored and if a player is standing in an offside position.

The referee also controls behaviour on the pitch and can penalise players and teams for bad, dangerous or unlawful play. His sanctions for serious breaches of the Laws are twofold. He can show a yellow card to a player to warn him his play is unacceptable or a red card, which results in the player being sent off the pitch immediately. Whenever the referee shows a card to a player, he makes a note in a notebook he keeps in his pocket, naming that player and the infringement in case there is an appeal after the match is over. If a player gets two yellow cards during a game, it automatically results in a red card being awarded, and he will be sent off.

The referee can also take advice from his assistants on bad behaviour he hasn't personally seen (for instance if a player hits another while his back is turned) and can award cards based on the assistants' advice.

If the referee sees or is made aware of an infringement of the Laws, he has several options as well as the award of cards. He can give

▫ a direct or indirect free kick

   or

▫ a penalty shot at goal.

Here, together with detailed explanations, are the standard hand signals used by referees and their assistants.

Direct free kick

(includes an indication of the direction/team who will take the kick)

A direct free kick is awarded when a player:

▫ Kicks or attempts to kick an opponent
▫ Trips or attempts to trip an opponent
▫ Jumps at an opponent
▫ Charges an opponent (including shoulder charges)
▫ Strikes or attempts to strike an opponent (including head butts)
▫ Pushes or shoves an opponent
▫ Makes contact with the opponent before touching the ball when tackling

◦ Holds an opponent
◦ Spits at an opponent
◦ Handles the ball deliberately (this includes the goalie outside his penalty area)

They should perhaps have included 'bites an opponent', but the penalties awarded against Luis Suarez for this offence in recent years have certainly made it clear that biting is not acceptable either.

If any of these offences are committed by a player inside their own penalty area, then it's a penalty kick. See our information on penalty kicks later in this section.

Curiously, if a team kicks a direct or an indirect free kick into its own goal, then a corner kick is awarded to the opposition rather than giving them an instant goal. It's pretty rare that this happens, of course.

A direct free kick is a simple move – a player from the team that was deprived of the ball is given back the ball to kick wherever he wants (including straight into the goal if he is close enough to do this).

No players from the opposing team are allowed to stand closer than 10 yards (9 m) away from the ball. This free-kick zone allows the kicker greater freedom to use the ball without challenge. If the kick is being taken close to the goal (just on the edge of the penalty area, for instance), opposing defenders will form a wall to protect the goalkeeper and the goal.

One of the funnier sights for those watching a game, the wall always takes some time to arrange, with one member of the wall facing the goalie to check where he wants them to stand, before turning round to face the kicker alongside his team-mates.

Walls can be made up of several players but are generally between three and five strong. Once their position is approved by the goalie, all the members of the wall will face the kicker, and boys usually place their hands down in front of their most sensitive parts to protect them from the hurtling ball being aimed in their direction.

The boys' wall – interesting to compare with the girls' wall on page 88

Members of the attacking side may also try to join the wall, just to confuse, and this is a clever ruse as they can wait until their team-mate kicks the ball and then move to one side, making a space in the wall for the ball to come through towards the goal.

Obviously a lot of jostling takes place as the players line up and get ready for the kick, and depending on how quickly this gets out of hand, further disciplinary action may be taken by the referee. It's quite a fine line between defending your right to stand on the pitch in a particular position and pushing an opponent over.

It seems the most natural reaction from the defenders to the oncoming ball is to jump up in the air – presumably they think they may be able to head it away or perhaps they're just trying to avoid getting hit. Whatever the reason, the ball could quite easily disappear towards the goal under their jumping feet which would certainly surprise the goalkeeper, but this rarely happens as balls tend to rise in the air when kicked.

The kicker is only allowed to touch the ball once before another player touches it; no double kicks are allowed by the person taking the free kick.

Ever since the 2014 World Cup, referees have used a new technique to mark the 10-yard distance from the free-kick ball, using a white vanishing aerosol foam to spray a line on the ground behind which defending players must stand. This ensures they keep 10 yards (9 m) away from the kicker, and the foam degrades and disappears in a couple of minutes to leave the pitch clear for further play. Having proved so successful during that World Cup competition, this system is now in use across all types of football. The foam is also used to mark the spot from which a free kick must be taken – this has been very helpful in stopping players moving the ball further towards the goal once a kick has been awarded.

Indirect free kick

(as before, the referee will indicate which team should take the kick)

Indirect free kicks are awarded when a player:

◦ Impedes the progression of an opponent (obstruction)
◦ Plays in a dangerous manner (e.g., high tackles)
◦ Prevents the goalkeeper from releasing the ball from his hands

Or when a keeper, inside their own penalty area:

◦ Holds on to the ball for more than 6 seconds
◦ Handles a back pass
◦ Handles the ball after receiving it from a team-mate directly from a throw-in
◦ Touches the ball (with hands) before it is touched by another player, having previously released it from their possession

When taking an indirect free kick, a player from the team that was deprived of the ball is given it back but cannot kick it directly into the goal. It must touch at least one other player (from either side) before a goal can be scored. Again, the opposing players must stand at least 10 yards (9 m) away from the ball and may form a wall as they do for a direct free kick.

Drop ball

If play is halted, for an injury to a player or a pitch invasion by an animal or a fan, for instance, it would be unfair to restart without allowing both teams to compete for the ball, so a drop-ball restart is the solution.

The referee will call one player from each side to stand in front of him and will drop the ball between them, and they can then compete to take control of the ball. Drop balls that would otherwise occur in the goal area are taken from a point on the line parallel to the goal line nearest to where the incident occurred; they cannot be taken farther inside the goal area. The same rule applies to indirect free kicks taken in the goal area.

Occasionally you will see that in the spirit of fair play, if a player is injured during the game, and a *drop ball* or *throw-in* is awarded to his opposition, the players who would gain an unfair advantage will pass the ball straight back to the other team to allow them to continue as if the game had not been halted for the injury.

Penalty kick

As we explained earlier, a penalty kick is awarded when an infringement that would otherwise result in a direct free kick takes place within the penalty area.

The penalty shot is usually taken by the member of the team who is best qualified to take penalties. Every team has a player who excels in this role, and naturally they are valuable members of the team.

Once a player has been nominated to take the kick, the ball is placed on the penalty spot inside the penalty area, and all the other players must stand outside the area as the penalty is taken. You will remember this includes standing outside the D at the edge of the penalty area to ensure all players are standing at least 10 yards (9 m) away from the ball until the kick is taken.

The referee will then blow his whistle once to advise the kicker that the shot can be taken. The goalkeeper is allowed to move about on his goal line ahead of the shot being taken to try to distract the penalty kicker. Once the ball has been kicked, the other players are allowed to return to the area, and if the penalty rebounds, either off the woodwork or from the goalkeeper, they can attack or defend again. The term *goalmouth scramble* very effectively describes what happens after a penalty is taken and missed, as all the defending players dash to help the goalkeeper clear his line while the attackers scramble to get to the ball and try to score.

Yellow card and red card

As we've already explained, some punishments from the referee also involve showing cards. Yellow cards will be shown for the following offences:

◦ Anything that can be deemed as unsporting behaviour
◦ Dissent by word or action
◦ Persistent infringement of the Laws – for example, a series of fouls
◦ Delaying the restart of play – for example, by kicking the ball away
◦ Not retreating the required distance at a free kick or corner
◦ Entering or re-entering the pitch without the referee's permission
◦ Deliberately leaving the pitch without the referee's permission

Red cards are shown either to players whose offence is so bad they will be sent from the pitch and miss the remainder of the game or to players getting a second yellow card in a match who will also be shown a red card and told to leave the pitch immediately. In simple terms, two yellow cards equal a red card.

Throw-in (assistant referee signal)

When the ball goes off the pitch at the *sidelines*, teams can select any player to throw it back in. That player can then pick up the ball and throw it back onto the pitch, ideally at the feet or head of another player from his team.

Goal kick

If the ball goes off the field behind the goal line from an attacking player, the goalkeeper's team is awarded a goal kick, and it usually falls to the goalkeeper to clear the ball away from his goal area. These huge clearance kicks can start attacking moves for his team if he succeeds in linking up with attackers close to the opposition penalty area.

Goal kicks are also awarded if the attacking team kicks an indirect free kick directly into the goal.

Corner kick

If the ball goes behind the goal line after touching a defender (including the goalkeeper), the attacking team is awarded a corner kick. The ball is placed in the arc next to the corner flag and kicked from there by a player from the attacking team.

Corner kicks often result in goals being scored when the players jostle with their opposition to get to the ball and shoot at goal, and of course goalkeepers sometimes join the attackers, too, to provide that extra height *in the box*, either to head the ball directly into goal or down towards their forwards.

Advantage

(the referee indicates which direction the team awarded the ball is playing)

This signal shows both teams that despite an infringement having taken place, assuming the team that would have been given a free kick gains possession of the ball, that team is allowed to continue its attack on the basis that halting the game would actually penalise them further instead of helping them. The referee will continue to hold out his arm for a short period of time to demonstrate that advantage is being played and will drop his arm once the advantage period has elapsed.

If a team has gained an advantage initially but their subsequent attack is rapidly halted by the opposition, the referee (having called advantage) will return to the spot of the original infringement and award a free kick from that point.

This can be somewhat confusing for a new spectator who sees an offence being committed but play continues regardless and then play gets stopped a few minutes later, and all the players move back to the position where the original foul occurred, which to a newcomer can often look like a random part of the pitch. If this happens while you're watching, you can be pretty certain the referee was playing advantage.

Offside (assistant referee signal)

If the assistant referee (linesman) gives this sign, the referee will know a player was standing offside during a particular move. The assistant referee will also hold his flag at specific heights to indicate the positioning of the offside player. Position one in our diagram indicates that a player on the far side of the pitch was standing offside.

For a player offside in the centre of the pitch, the flag is held out with an outstretched arm at shoulder height. Finally, for a player on the side of the pitch closest to the assistant referee, the flag is pointed down in position 3 on our diagram.

In this way, the referee immediately knows which player caused the offside flag to be raised and can ensure the free kick is taken from the correct location on the pitch.

Substitution (assistant referee signal)

This signal is the one the assistant referee uses to tell the referee a substitution has been requested.

Numbers of substitutes allowed at matches vary considerably. In a top-flight game, seven subs are allowed to be named for each team, but only three can be used to actually substitute for the players who start of the game on the pitch.

In *friendly* matches, unlimited numbers can be named and as many changes can be made. Sometimes at international friendly matches, the whole starting 11 can be changed for the second half of the match. In school matches, teams rarely have more than a couple of substitutes, one attacker and one defender, and they only get to play in the event of an injury to one of their team members or if the school team coach thinks they should get *a run out* towards the end of the match.

The infamous offside law

'Fair enough, he was in an offside position, but I don't think he was offside.'

(Jimmy Greaves)

Infamous? Well it certainly causes more controversy and conversation than just about any other aspect of the game. And yes, we know it's madness to try to explain the offside law to non-players, but we're going to give it our best shot (yet another football cliché!).

At its simplest, any player standing ahead of the ball and the last defender (apart from the goalie) when the ball is played to him by a team-mate is deemed to be offside. The most important thing to note is that he must be standing ahead of the ball as it is played (i.e. closer to the goal that his team are attacking).

In the original 1863 laws, a player was offside unless three players from the opposing side were in front of him (including the goalie).

In 1925, this was changed so that a player was deemed offside with two players in front of him when he received the ball (one of those players being the goalie).

In 1990, another amendment was made which stated that players standing in line with an opposition defender would be considered onside, and it was probably this change that has made judging offside so much more difficult for the officials.

In 2005, FIFA added the active rule to the law, and subsequent changes in 2013 meant that players can be standing in an offside position but not actually be deemed offside. Of course that sounds like complete nonsense at first, but let's see if we can explain it.

Here's a simple explanation in diagrammatic form:

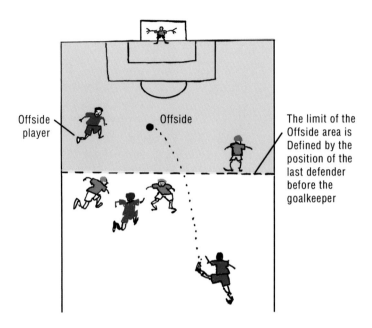

As you can see from the diagram, the second last opponent is the player who determines where the offside area begins, and it can be anywhere in his half of the pitch. The referee's assistant is responsible for checking and making decisions based on this offside area. It sounds perfectly simple doesn't it, but just you wait!

The change to the law meant that a player can stand in an offside position provided they are not 'actively involved in play' or 'interfering with play'. It was meant to encourage attacking football but instead is very open to interpretation and, most importantly, human error, so it results in more arguments than pretty much anything else in football.

FIFA recently qualified the original description by clarifying that 'interfering with play means *playing or touching* the ball passed or touched by a team-mate', which seems pretty clear cut. However, a player doesn't necessarily have to touch the ball to *influence* play. So they can still be offside if (in the opinion of the referee or his assistant) they are either interfering with an opponent or gaining an advantage for themselves or their team.

What on earth does that mean? Apparently, if an attacker is standing in an offside position and interferes with an opponent by either preventing them from playing or being able to play the ball by either clearly obstructing their line of vision or movements or by making a gesture of movement which deceives or distracts that opponent, while standing in a potentially offside position, then they will be judged offside.

For example, if the ball gets played into the penalty area and the offside player plays the ball after it rebounds off a post, crossbar or an opposing defender, then he will be deemed offside as he will have gained an advantage by being in that position.

Just to clarify, you *can't* be offside if:

◦ You receive the ball directly from a goal kick, a throw-in or a corner kick (hence the packed penalty area during corner kicks)
◦ You are in your own half of the pitch
◦ You are level with the second last or last two opponents
◦ You are level with or behind the ball
◦ You are not actively involved in play (as we explained)
◦ You receive the ball from a member of the opposition
◦ You receive the ball after it has hit the goal woodwork (having been standing in an onside position when the ball was originally kicked)

If the referee believes an offside offence has occurred, he awards an indirect free kick to the opposing team, which must be taken from the place where the infringement happened.

Goodness, you have to feel sorry for the referees these days, don't you? Making the call on an offside player is fraught with difficulties that few imagined when the original law was created.

Hopefully this will clarify why there's so much controversy over these decisions, even if you're still just as confused about when a player is actually deemed to be offside.

Here's our attempt to show an offside situation under the current Laws.

Player A is delivering the ball by passing it into the area just outside the penalty area. Player D is the last defender who defines the edge of the offside area. Player C, although currently standing in an offside position in strict terms, is not influencing play and is therefore NOT offside. Player B is onside, and if he moves to pick up the pass and scores, it will all be legal. If player C runs in and connects with the ball, however, he will be deemed offside (having been standing in an offside position as the ball was delivered).

If you'd like to see more graphical representations of the possible offside positions, you can find them in FIFA's detailed explanation here:

>> www.fifa.com/mm/document/footballdevelopment/refereeing/02/36/01/11/27_06_2014_new--lawsofthegameweben_neutral.pdf

and the FA's version here:

>> www.thefa.com/football-rules-governance/laws/football-11-11/law-11---offside.aspx

FIFA used to claim it's as simple as 1, 2, 3, but their explanation then took up over 30 interactive pages of diagrams and descriptions. Perhaps that goes some way towards confirming our feeling that it's really pretty complicated to understand. The latest edition of the Laws (published for the 2014-15 season) still take 18 pages to explain the law.

And here's their explanation of the changes to the law in 2013 – we're not sure it's any clearer at all, but that's the joy of the English language:

INTERFERING – what the law used to say:

'Interfering with play' means playing or touching the ball passed or touched by a team-mate.

'Interfering with an opponent' means preventing an opponent from playing or being able to play the ball by clearly obstructing the opponent's line of vision or movement or making a gesture or movement which, in the opinion of the referee, deceives or distracts an opponent.

INTERFERING – what the law now says:

'Interfering with play' means playing or touching the ball passed or touched by a team-mate.

'Interfering with an opponent' means preventing an opponent from playing or being able to play the ball by clearly obstructing the opponent's line of vision or movement or challenging an opponent for the ball.

GAINING AN ADVANTAGE – what the law used to say:

'Gaining an advantage by being in that position' means playing a ball that rebounds to him off a goal post or the crossbar having been in an offside position or playing a ball that rebounds to him off an opponent having been in an offside position.

GAINING AN ADVANTAGE – what the law now says:

'Gaining an advantage by being in that position' means playing a ball…

That rebounds or is deflected to him off the goal post, crossbar or an opponent having been in an offside position.

That rebounds, is deflected or is played to him from a deliberate save by an opponent having been in an offside position.

It's worth noting that a player standing in a potentially offside position and receiving the ball from an opponent who deliberately plays the ball to him (except for a deliberate save by the goalie) is not considered to have gained an advantage. In other words, you can be standing in an offside position, and if a defender kicks the ball to you, you're not offside! Gosh, they don't make this easy for the referee, do they?

Of course, defenders can use the offside law to try to trap strikers offside. They wait until a free kick is just about to be taken and then, to trap the attackers offside, they move away from their goal area leaving the attackers offside as the ball is struck. Well-drilled defences get very skilled at this and are able to catch their opponents offside on a regular basis.

We hope this all helps, but rest assured even when you do think you are in total command of Law 11, referee decisions will baffle you as much as the rest of the crowd and commentators. If you hear complaints about offside decisions, don't be surprised. Human error is a wonderful thing, and without it, post-match analysis would really be quite boring.

Goal line technology/Goal Decision System

'That goal surprised most people, least of all myself.'
(Garth Crooks)

'He scored! There's no end to the stoppages of this drama.'
(Alan Parry)

Modern technology can help out the officials to ensure accurate decisions during a game, and goal-line technology is a good example of what's now available. It might help, but we're pretty much convinced it won't actually stop all the arguments, and certainly not at junior level where it won't be in use.

The whole idea of the newly-approved goal decision system is to ensure that when the ball crosses the goal line, a goal is properly awarded to the scoring team. You may have seen it in full action during the 2014 World Cup competition.

Sometimes during goal mouth clashes, the game is moving so fast and with so many players involved that neither the referee nor his assistants are able to see if the ball actually crosses the line or not.

Simple television replays don't always catch the right angle either, so despite constant experimentation with this form of review, the football authorities have now approved similar technology to that used at tennis and cricket matches.

Tests took place around the world to check several systems and their accuracy before the Goal Decision System (GDS) was chosen. In April 2013, the Hawk-Eye system used in tennis and cricket was approved for use in football, and all 20 Premier League clubs in England and Wales now have the system installed at their grounds.

Hawk-Eye consists of seven cameras, operating at 340 frames per second, compared with TV's 25 frames. When the ball crosses the plane of the goal, a signal is sent to all four match officials either through an earpiece or via a watch which will vibrate, beep and display the text 'goal'. That signal is relayed to the officials within a second of the event, and broadcasters are able to display the decision via a virtual representation within 20 seconds.

It is hoped that this technology will reduce the few match-changing errors made by the officials at important matches (there were just 31 such decisions made during the 2012-13 Premiership season, for instance).

For the vast majority of games that are played without the benefit of this additional technology, however, the teams will continue to rely solely on the eyes of the referee and his assistants, and the arguments will no doubt persist.

A girls' team wall – spot the differences from the boys on page 70

Supporters' work

'There's no mud without flames.'

(Gordon Taylor)

Family supporters are an unsung breed who care for and nurture the nation's footballers. If you're in the States, you might be known as a Soccer Mom or Dad. We understand that as a parent or grandparent (or perhaps as a partner) your role will probably revolve around the mundane things like cleaning kit and providing the family taxi cab service to and from matches.

Getting kitted out

One of your most important roles in helping your young players to start their love affair with the beautiful game is helping them to buy their first football kit. This will consist of a pair (or two) of socks, shorts, shirts and, most importantly, *shin pads* and boots.

Kids play football in their trainers and school shoes quite happily, but if they're going to take the game seriously, they'll need the proper kit. Our first recommendation is not to allow them to wear their favourite team colours for recreational football. Buy them a T-shirt in similar colours to their team by all means, but keep their very expensive replica shirt for wearing out socially, not for playing in and getting muddy.

Replica shirts have become big business, with the world's leading teams changing their *strip* every season, usually both home and away kit, so keeping your keen football fan up to date can cost a small fortune. Wearing last year's shirt is just not acceptable for the real footie fan – it's not an abbreviation for the word 'fanatic' for nothing.

Children grow rapidly and will outgrow each season's shirt anyway, so it will be an expensive business keeping them up to date if they support one of the Premier League teams.

Team kits

If your kid joins a school or club team, they will need the team kit, which will include shirt, socks and shorts. Luckily whatever football boots they own can be used in all games, as can their shin pads. Most schools and clubs have a second-hand shop or sales system you can access, not necessarily for their match-day kit, but at least for a set of kit for practices.

So many clubs (and schools) plan practices for the day before the game, and despite modern fabrics making washing and drying kit simpler these days, it's so much easier to have a second set for your player to use at the practice and then a set of clean kit ready for use on match day.

Boots

Choosing the right boots for your little player is fraught with complications. Football boots used to be high-sided, heavy leather, traditional working men's boots with hard studs permanently embedded in them. Modern football boots are much lighter and closer to trainers in design. However, the manufacturers make it complicated for you by having separate soft ground, hard ground, artificial pitch and indoor boots.

Prices for kids vary from £25 to £100 for a pair of boots. Hopefully you will find an all-round boot that will allow your player to play on standard grass pitches, and they can use their usual trainers indoors unless they become serious team players.

Advising you which boots to buy would be foolish. Just go along to your favourite sports supply shop and get your child to try some on. Get them to walk about in them and make sure they feel comfy when moving fast, not just slowly – they're going to be running around in these boots after all. Celebrity-endorsed boots are not guaranteed to be any better than the standard boots made by the same manufacturer, but pester power means that many parents will succumb to buying them as presents for Christmas or birthdays. Once your young player has a regular position, particular types of boot may be preferable, but again your local sports shop will be able to advise you.

Shin pads

Shin pads come in various styles, too. Again, the position being played will influence choosing these. Prices vary considerably – from £10 to £75 for a pair. The days when a young player stuffed his short shin pads inside his socks and hoped they would stay in place are long gone, and specially fitted sleeves are now worn inside the socks that will keep the pads in place. The pads are even ergonomically designed to fit right and left legs separately. This style of pad is much easier to wear and will ensure saggy socks don't allow the slip-in style of pad to fall out and get lost during a game.

Bear in mind that fast-running players will prefer the lighter-weight ones, while defenders will want all the protection available and may opt for something sturdier.

Goalkeeper gloves

Helping your young goalie choose the best gloves will be vital if they are to succeed in this role. However, some manufacturers don't help with some gloves for kids for an age range of 8 to 15! It's well worth hunting for the ones that make individual sizes so that you can change them from season to season and ensure your little goalie has the best chance possible of stopping goals without fear of injury.

Your local sports shop staff will be happy to help you choose the best ones, so never be afraid to ask.

Taxi service

With the arrival of satellite navigation devices and online mapping systems, getting to the right ground for a match is less fraught than it used to be, but if your team coach or the school teacher in charge doesn't give you a postcode and you have to search for a ground, it's always worth asking more senior members of the club or school supporters for help, as they may well have been to a ground before with older children.

Helping to get a team to a game is one of the most rewarding things parents can do when raising their kids. You get to meet your child's friends and team-mates, and your support is always appreciated. It's a great chance to bond with the younger generation and something we can thoroughly recommend to you.

At home games, you might get asked to help with half-time refreshments or teas, but generally football games are less formal than rugby or cricket, and teams just head home once the match is over, frequently still covered in mud. Having an old rug (or two) to cover your car seats can be really useful for the return journey!

Do make sure your charges change out of their boots before scrambling into your car, which can be very tempting if it's raining and they want to get warm and dry. At least that way the filthy, muddy boots can sit in your car boot and not deposit the mud all over your clean car on the journey home.

Cleaning kit

There's nothing very magical about cleaning football kit these days. With pre-soak programmes in washing machines and effective stain removers, it's a much simpler task than it was a couple of generations ago.

If the kit has been allowed to dry out, it's well worth soaking it in a bucket of cold water before putting it into the washing machine. You can add some stain remover (we love Vanish for its simple yet effective action), and it will certainly help to ensure the kit comes out like new after a standard cool wash. Always check the washing labels on kit before putting it in, though; some fabrics just don't like temperatures over 30° C or 40° C, and this is especially true of socks.

Kits dry out fairly rapidly, but as we said earlier, we still recommend having two sets to cover those days when practice happens in the evening before a match on the following day.

Boots present different challenges. Of course they can be scrubbed under the tap, and we recommend you keep a separate nail brush by your kitchen or utility room sink just for this purpose. However, if they're made of leather, then they need to be dried really carefully – putting a pair of wet football boots on a radiator will result in crusty leather that is very uncomfortable to wear and might even shrink the boots. Stuffing them with dry newspaper is a traditional technique.

You then leave them somewhere warm overnight (an airing cupboard is perfect), but if you don't have one of these, just leave them close to a radiator but not on it. If you're in a hurry, a hairdryer set on medium/low (definitely not hot) will work quite well.

Modern boots are frequently coated in plastic to make them more waterproof, but this will crack after use, and some are now made from lightweight synthetic leather so need less maintenance than fully leather boots. However, if you've just bought a new pair of leather boots, you might want to consider waxing them to make them last longer. You can still dubbin boots – dubbin, I hear you say, who uses that these days? And where can I buy it? Well of course your local sports shop should stock it or its modern equivalent, and your local camping/climbing shop certainly will, and it really does work extremely well, that much we can guarantee.

Dubbing wax, or dubbin, is designed to maximise water repellence, offer protection from dirt and stains and keep leather supple. And if you're not sure how to apply dubbin to your leather boots or shoes for the best result, here's how:

1. Ensure that leather boots or shoes are clean before applying dubbin.

2. While heat will help the wax penetrate the leather easier, it is important not to apply direct heat to your boot as this can cause the leather to dry out and split. A hairdryer can be used to heat up your shoes or boots until warm – do not overheat and never leave your shoes near a radiator or open fire to heat up. If the wax is too hard to rub in, this can be warmed up in the same way.

3. Apply a small amount of dubbin to a cloth and rub evenly over the leather. Dubbing wax will leave a slightly oily film on leather (important for repelling water and dirt) and as such should be applied sparingly.

4. Leave for 30 to 60 minutes.

5. Buff off with a dry cloth.

6. Repeat as many times as necessary, ensuring wax is spread evenly and sparingly each time.

So now you're all set. Clean kit and boots along with good shin pads are all your little players will need to be ready to play. A track suit to keep them warm before and after the match is a good idea, and most teams have a team or school track suit to use these days.

Make sure you mark it carefully with their name, though – track suits (and general kits for that matter) have a nasty habit of 'walking' if they are not well marked.

If you have embroidery skills, it's well worth sewing a large set of initials, or a nickname or number, in matching colour cotton or silk onto the back of the track suit top to ensure it only gets worn by your child.

You just need to kit yourself out now with a warm coat, winter woollies, scarf, gloves, hat and probably an umbrella or waterproof poncho, too. We thoroughly recommend wearing walking or Wellington boots to the match. The field will undoubtedly be muddy, and wearing your good shoes to watch your offspring play will probably ruin them. You will almost certainly want to wander up and down the sideline to see them at close quarters, and fashion shoes just won't survive for long.

If you regularly go to watch your son or daughter play after work, try to keep a pair of old shoes in your car or at work so you can change into them before stepping onto that muddy field.

In the next section, we'll introduce you to the concept of Respect in football. As a new supporter, it's vital you learn about how to behave well at a match, and this Football Association initiative is keen to ensure football supporters all behave appropriately nowadays.

Apart from being embarrassing for your young player, your behaviour reflects on the whole team and their reputation in their local football community – worth bearing in mind when you're tempted to scream abuse at the opposition or the match officials out of frustration or anger at the actions of someone on the pitch.

Fair play, respect and supporters' etiquette

'England has the best fans in the world, and Scotland's fans are second to none.'

(Kevin Keegan)

Fair play in football

Alongside the Laws of the game, FIFA advocates a Fair Play programme. This is based around a number of rules, typically involving abstract ideas, but intended to inform footballers and spectators on proper behaviour both on and off the field:

- Play fair on the field
- Play to win but accept defeat properly
- Observe the Laws of the Game
- Respect everyone involved in the game
- Promote football's interests
- Honour those who defend football's reputation
- Reject any corruption, drugs, racism, violence and other harmful vices
- Help others to do exactly the same
- Denounce any who discredits the integrity of football
- Use football to make a better world

These are certainly laudable aims, and we can only hope that in the coming years both football crowds and players get the message and the historic battles of the past are just that. The FA is doing its best to help this happen with its new Respect programme, too.

Respect

Football passions run high, and the politest of people can fall into a rage when playing or watching the game. Historically it has been known to bring about remarkable political turnarounds – the national team brokered a truce in Cote D'Ivoire during that country's civil war in 2006. However, it is also widely considered to have brought about the so-called 'football war' in June 1969 between El Salvador and Honduras, and football is believed to have raised tensions at the beginning of the Yugoslav wars of the 1990s, when a match in 1990 between Dinamo Zagreb and Red Star Belgrade degenerated into rioting. It's a game that arouses passions in so many ways.

It was a series of high profile incidents involving violence from both players and crowd that resulted in the introduction of the Respect initiative in 2008. This was launched in response to widespread concern about some of the behaviour that was being witnessed at all levels of football. The Respect programme was launched at the start of the 2008/09 season, and although much of the concern focused on the high profile incidents, there were other important issues which the programme aimed to address.

These were:

◊ To recruit and retain enough referees for the demands of the game at every level
◊ To reduce the number of assaults on referees
◊ To achieve an improvement in on-field player discipline, particularly in the area of dissent to referees
◊ To manage a step change in youth football on what is acceptable or unacceptable behaviour from parents and spectators at matches [this is where you come in!]

The FA were also keen to stress that progress against these objectives is only likely to be achieved with a recognition that respect is the collective responsibility of everyone involved in football to try to ensure that the game is fair, safe and enjoyable for all.

Now at the end of its fifth season, some of the outcomes of the Respect programme are encouraging, although with the conviction of spectators for a vicious attack on a referee at an amateur match in June 2013, there is still a long way to go. Those involved in the game are keen to point out that it is a programme, not a campaign. It is a marathon, not a sprint.

The programme echoes the work in other team sports where the Spirit of the Game initiative in cricket has brought about major changes in player behaviour, and the Core Values initiative in rugby is hoping to do the same in that sport for both players and supporters.

As a new football supporter, we hope you will take all this advice on board and become one of the new breed – passionate, caring and considerate. It's such a shame that this exciting sport can be marred by just a few loutish actions or remarks, and learning to respect players, officials and fellow supporters will go a long way to ensuring everyone enjoys the match to the full without incident.

If you demonstrate respect, your little player should follow suit, and the future of football as a family sport will be assured.

Kick it out

A major part of the UK Respect programme is an initiative originally called Let's Kick Racism Out of Football, now known simply as *Kick It Out*. The nature of fans' chanting, and indeed some behaviour from players themselves, has become more offensive to the general public over the years, and a major attempt is now being made to clean up football in terms of racist abuse towards players and fans alike. It is run by a small charity and works throughout the football, education and community sectors to challenge discrimination, encourage inclusive practices and campaign for positive change. It has close links with FIFA, UEFA and the Football Against Racism in Europe (FARE) network.

Sadly, rival international fans are still causing problems and incidents, like the one involving so-called Chelsea fans on the Paris Metro in February 2015, demonstrating that there's still a long way to go.

You can find all about the programme here:

≫ www.kickitout.org/about/

Let's hope all those working to clean up football's reputation succeed in creating a safe, friendly environment for everyone involved in this widely-loved game.

'Every seat has a bottom on it, and they've made some noise in here tonight.'

(John Rawling)

It's a fan's life

It's difficult for some to understand the immense passion that football arouses in its most fervent supporters, or fans, as they are rightly known. We mentioned this earlier in relation to the ancient versions of the game that could involve a whole village playing against their neighbours, and this has continued right up to the creation of the Premier League. The game is certainly tribal in the way locals from a town support their local team. Men, in particular, just don't swap allegiance when it comes to football teams. To this day, if you grow up in a particular town or city, that first team you support will become your team for life. However, things are changing.

Since the creation of the Premier League and the other national top-flight leagues, football has become big business, and this has started to change loyalties. You will find Manchester United or Real Madrid supporters all over the world. People from other cities and towns support the major clubs and wear their replica strips with pride. This of course means you're as likely to run into a rival team supporter on holiday abroad as in the next town.

We're not sure if the fighting and violence that became associated with football in the middle of the 20th century was as a result of these changes or not, but fans certainly became more violent. Policing football matches, which had been a popular volunteer duty for officers in the early part of the century, became something they dreaded as the century came to a close. In recent years, severe incidents seem to have been in decline, so perhaps the Respect programme and other measures are beginning to bear fruit.

History teaches us that football can heal wounds, too – just think back to the matches played on Christmas Day 1914 between German and British soldiers at the front in Flanders. There's more about these in our history section at the end of this book.

Following your team – wearing the team colours

True fans love to wear their replica team football T-shirts and other kit, both to watch their team play and generally out and about to demonstrate their support. Team strips come in all shades, colours and designs, and as we've already pointed out, in the Premier League they are changed every season as part of the commercial enterprise of the clubs involved.

Sales of replica strips provide a major income stream for all top-flight clubs across the world. Kitting out your young fan to support his team will probably set you back up to £100, depending on their age. Prices start around £42 for a short-sleeved shirt in the smallest size and go on up! Even shorts start at around £20.

Learning the team song

Curiously, music forms a major part of sporting competitions these days, and it's interesting to note that Rapid Vienna has its own fans' orchestra, while African stadiums pulsate to the sound of drums. The England team is followed by a brass band, which regularly entertains the crowd with a rendition of the theme from *The Great Escape.*

Music can act as a catalyst for supportive singing – Liverpool's anthem 'You'll Never Walk Alone' stands out here – but music can also be used to calm tempers. If you attend a top-flight match, you will certainly get to hear lots of music while you are there, not all of it in the original versions of course. Some of the words to the songs will have been altered by the fans to suit their team players' names ... and sometimes the language can get a little 'fruity', but it's all part of the fun of attending a football match.

Every team has its own song, varying from West Ham's 'I'm Forever Blowing Bubbles' to Crystal Palace's 'Glad All Over'. You will find it hard to resist joining in with anything from 'Here we go, Here we go, Here we go', to 'the referee's a w***er'. Just keep the message of the Respect programme in mind! We've listed the top 10 football chants from a 2014 survey below:

1. 'His name is Rio, and he watches from the stand' West Ham fans to Manchester United's Rio Ferdinand, sung to the tune of Duran Duran's 'Rio'.

2. 'When you're sat in row Z, and the ball hits your head, that's Zamora, that's Zamora' Fulham supporters hail their striker Bobby Zamora, sung to the tune of Dean Martin's 'That's Amore'.

3. 'You should have stayed on the telly' Newcastle United fans to Alan Shearer, when the Match of the Day pundit led the team to relegation as manager.

4. 'He's fast, he's red, he talks like Father Ted, Robbie Keane' Liverpool fans on the club's striker.

5. 'Your teeth are offside, your teeth are offside, Luis Suárez, your teeth are offside' Manchester United fans singing about former Liverpool player Luis Suárez.

6. 'Deep fry yer pizzas, we're gonna deep fry yer pizzas' Scotland fans to Italy's supporters in a World Cup qualifier in March 2007.

7. 'Chelsea, wherever you may be, keep your wife from John Terry' Chelsea fans saluted their captain Terry after his affair with former team-mate Wayne Bridge's ex-girlfriend, sung to the tune of 'Lord Of The Dance'.

8. 'John Carew, Carew. He likes a lap-dance or two. He might even pay for you. John Carew, Carew' Aston Villa fans sang this about their player to the 'Que Sera, Sera' song.

9. 'Fat Eddie Murphy, you're just a fat Eddie Murphy' Newcastle United fans used this heckle on then-Chelsea player Jimmy Floyd Hasselbaink.

10. 'You only live round the corner' Fulham to Manchester United supporters, a chant now sung by many other London teams when they play at home to United.

Finally, if you've caught the football bug, there are hundreds if not thousands of Internet sites devoted to football fans, and you could even play Fantasy Football, where you choose your own team from the leading players around the world and compete against other fantasy teams in an online competition. Look at:

» fantasy.premierleague.com/

The World Cup and other competitions

'The World Cup – truly an international event.'

(John Motson)

The World Cup is an international men's football tournament. The competition was first staged in 1930 in Uruguay, and it has been played every four years since, with the exception of a gap between 1938 and 1950 around the Second World War.

The 2014 competition was the 20th, and Brazil was hosting it for the second time (they first hosted the World Cup in 1950). You'd have to be pretty insulated from news reporting not to notice when a World Cup competition is taking place. The radio, TV, newspapers and other media become totally obsessed for the few weeks it takes place. The next competition will be held in Russia in 2018, and preliminary matches are already taking place with teams from over 200 countries around the world.

Eventually, national teams from 32 different countries will go through a qualification competition to be part of the tournament.

Germany, the 2014 World Cup winners, beat Argentina in the final, 1-0, breaking a long-lasting tradition that competitions held in South America were always won by South American teams.

If you feel you understand a bit more about the game now, we know you'll enjoy watching matches on TV or listening to some commentary on the radio.

The World Cup competition is guaranteed to amuse, entertain and outrage football supporters the world over. If you're buying this book ahead of the next competition, we hope you'll enjoy it even more once you've absorbed all this information.

There are many other club and national competitions being held across the world. Some are annual, some less frequent, but they include the UEFA Cup, the European Cup, the Oceania Cup, CONCACAF, African Cup, Asian Cup, and South America has several competitions.

FIFA organises the Women's World Cup, the FIFA Confederations Cup and unofficially the Summer Olympic Games competition. They also promote U-20 and U-17 World Cups for both men and women, as well as the youth Olympic games and the FIFA Club World Cup.

In Japan and South America, there is the Suruga Bank Championship. In the Arab world, the Arab Cup of Nations, the Pan Arab Games and the Gulf Cup of Nations. In Asia there's the Asian Cup, the AFC Champions League, the AFC Cup and the AFC President's Cup.

In Africa, national teams play in the Africa Cup of Nations, the All-Africa Games (U-23 players), U-20s play in the African Youth Championship, and there's also an U-17 Championship. Clubs compete in the CAF Champions League, the CAF Confederation Cup and the CAF Super Cup.

For North America, Central American and the Caribbean region (known as CONCACAF), there is the CONCACAF Gold Cup, the UNCAF Nations Cup and the Caribbean Cup. Their clubs play for the CONCACAF Champions League, UNCAF Club Tournament and the CFU Club Championship.

The South American nations have the Copa América and the Superclásico de las Américas, and clubs compete in the Copa Libertadores (and its female equivalent), the Copa Sudamericana and the Recopa Sudamericana.

In Oceania there's the OFC Nations Cup, and for clubs the OFC Champions League. In Europe where UEFA organises most of the competitions, there are so many it's almost scary.

Here's a list of current competitions being played.

UEFA European Football Championship	National teams	Each 4 years (doubly even years)
UEFA Regions' Cup	Sub-national teams	Each 2 years (odd years)
UEFA Super Cup	Super cup	Each year (August); between UEFA Champions League and UEFA Europa League winners (clubs)
UEFA Champions League	1st-tier cup	Each year (September→May) (clubs)
UEFA Europa League	2nd-tier cup	Each year (September→May). Known as UEFA Cup 1971–2009 (clubs)
4 Associations' Tournament	Sub-continental cup	Each 2 years (odd years) starting in 2011, between the men's national teams of Northern Ireland, the Republic of Ireland, Scotland and Wales
Baltic League	Sub-continental cup	Each year (March→November); between 4 Estonian, 4 Latvian and 4 Lithuanian clubs

Livonia Cup	Sub-continental cup	Each year (January); between the Estonian and Latvian club champions
Royal League	Sub-continental cup	Each year (November→April); between 4 Danish, 4 Norwegian and 4 Swedish clubs (the 2007–08 tournament was not held)
Setanta Sports Cup	Sub-continental cup	Each year (February→October); between 6 Irish and 6 Northern Irish clubs
Trofeo Colombina	Sub-continental cup	Each year (August); hosted by Recreativo de Huerlva, 2 or 3 European clubs are invited for each tournament
UEFA European U-21 Football Championship	U-21 teams	Each 2 years (odd years) (national teams)
UEFA European U-19 Football Championship	U-19 teams	Each year (July) (national teams)
UEFA Euoprean U-17 Football Championship	U-17 teams	Each year (May) (national teams)

UEFA Women's Championship	National teams	Each 4 years (years following doubly even years)
UEFA Women's Champions League	Continental Cup	Each year (August→May); known as UEFA Women's Cup 2001–09 (clubs)
UEFA Women's U-19 Championship	U-19 teams	Each year (July) (national teams)
UEFA Women's U-17 Championship	U-17 teams	Each year (May or June) (national teams)

Just to confound us, UEFA has just announced yet another major tournament for European countries entitled the League of Nations. It will start in September 2018 (after that year's World Cup is complete) and will provide four qualifying spots for the UEFA European Championship – the next one being Euro 2020.

All the countries taking part will be divided into four divisions, further divided into four smaller pools. The tournament will include promotion and relegation between the divisions and will replace most friendly fixtures.

The best four teams in each division who have not already qualified for Euro 2020 will play off for the final four places as part of the League of Nations tournament. It is planned to play the games in 13 cities around Europe.

On current ranking, the top division is likely to include Germany, Italy, Spain and England.

As you can see, competitions between clubs and countries take place all over the world throughout the year. For the keen football supporter, this means there's always something to watch somewhere in the world. If you don't want to become a football widow(er), you could do no better than use our guide to develop the same passion for the game as your family and friends, but we appreciate that for some of you the so-called 'summer break' can come as welcome relief from wall-to-wall football during the rest of the year.

National matches of course engender even greater fan activity and passion, and it's pretty much impossible to ignore your local national team's matches if they are involved in one of the major tournaments.

Throughout the world, national flags are hung in the streets and outside houses. Pubs, restaurants and cafés get behind their favourites and have special TV showings for fans to come along and join in the atmosphere of a crowd.

Others choose to have friends round and share a few beers while they watch the match. Communal match watching is great fun, and if you're beginning to understand more about the beautiful game now you've read this book, you'll probably enjoy this experience even more in the future.

Finally, we promised you some more detailed football history earlier in the book, and as we reach the end of our guide, here are those details. We hope you will find these other aspects of football's history as fascinating as we do.

A little bit more history

For those of you who enjoyed our first chapter with some of the early history of the game, here's more detail which will help to explain how the game developed and how it is now organised across the world.

After the recognition of football as a defined sport, games of football were played in public schools in England (these are private schools for those of you in the USA) and at their old boys' clubs and then of course at universities. The game was also played at informal clubs, and for many years each club or school team had its own set of rules.

This obviously made it difficult for teams to play against each other. In the 1800s, teams arriving at Cambridge University posted their individual rules on trees around the recreation area, but in 1848, two former Shrewsbury School pupils called a meeting at Trinity College with 12 other representatives from the famous public schools of Eton, Harrow, Rugby, Winchester and Shrewsbury. The meeting lasted over eight hours, but they came up with the first set of modern rules, now known as the *Cambridge Rules*.

No copy of these rules exists now, but a revised version dating from around 1856 is held in the library of Shrewsbury School. These rules clearly favour the kicking game over handling (although handling was allowed for a player to take a clean catch entitling them to a free kick), and there was a primitive offside rule, disallowing players from 'loitering' around the opponents' goal. The *Cambridge Rules* were not widely adopted outside the English public schools and universities, but they were probably the foundation for what we now know as the Laws of the Game.

In 1857, the first truly independent football club was created in Sheffield, called Sheffield Wednesday. Of course, it too had its own set of rules, including the wearing of hats to distinguish the teams from each other, which must have made heading the ball interesting!

Then during the early 1860s, there were increasing attempts in England to unify and reconcile the various public school games. In 1862, one J.C. Thring, who had been one of the driving forces behind the original Cambridge Rules and who was now a master at Uppingham School, issued his own rules of what he called 'The Simplest Game' (predictably these are also known as the 'Uppingham Rules').

In early October 1863, another new revised version of the Cambridge Rules was drawn up by a committee representing former pupils from Harrow, Shrewsbury, Eton, Rugby, Marlborough and Westminster.

Finally, on the evening of 26 October 1863 at the Freemason's Tavern in London's Great Queen Street, representatives of several leading football clubs met for the inaugural meeting of the Football Association (FA). The aim of the association was to establish a single unifying code and regulate the playing of the game among its members. Following the first meeting, the public schools were invited to join the association.

All of them declined, except Charterhouse and Uppingham. This might seem odd, but you have to remember that rugby football was a growing sport in most public schools at the time. Altogether, six meetings of the FA were held between October and December 1863, and after the third meeting, a draft set of rules was published.

At the beginning of the fourth meeting, attention was drawn to the recently published Cambridge Rules of 1863. The Cambridge Rules differed from the draft FA rules in two significant areas: (1) running with or carrying the ball, and (2) *hacking* (kicking opposing players in the shins).

At the fifth meeting, it was proposed that these two rules be removed. Most of the delegates supported this, but the representative from Blackheath, who was the first FA treasurer, objected. He was quoted as saying, 'hacking is the true football.' However, the motion to ban both running with the ball in hand and hacking was carried, and Blackheath then withdrew from the FA.

Its representative F.W. Campbell is also quoted as saying, 'If you do away with [hacking], I will be bound to bring over a lot of Frenchmen who would beat you with a week's practice.' Despite this threat, after that final meeting on 8 December 1863, the FA published the *Laws of Football*, the first comprehensive set of rules for the game.

In 1863, just 11 teams formed the Football Association. The clubs included some famous names that still exist in the English Football League today, including Notts County, Sheffield Wednesday and Preston North End.

It wasn't until 1870 that a dedicated goalkeeper had to be nominated for each team, and it took until 1877 for the first set of unified rules to be universally agreed for the now official game of Association Football. You can see the original Laws from 1863 in our earlier history section on page 20.

Since it was the very first football association in the world, the Football Association in England is the only one not to have a country name in its title. It is simply the FA. In France, they have the Fédération Française de

Football, and in Brazil, the Confederação Brasileira de Futebol, or CBF – the Brazilian Football Confederation.

As you might imagine, the power and influence of the British Empire in the late 19th century allowed the varying codes laid down by the public schools to spread to areas of British influence outside the directly-controlled Empire as their former pupils travelled to work around the Empire. By the end of that century, distinct regional codes were developing, including Australian rules, American and Gaelic football.

The Laws of the game are now overseen by the International Football Association Board which was first formed in 1886 at a meeting of the FA in Manchester, initially governing games between the four British Isles countries of England, Scotland, Ireland and Wales.

In 1888, the English Football League was formed, creating the first professional football clubs in the world and initiating regular competitions between those clubs. It was made up from just 12 teams from the Midlands and north of England.

In alphabetical order they were:

Accrington Stanley	Aston Villa
Blackburn Rovers	Bolton Wanderers
Burnley	Derby County
Everton	Notts County
Preston North End	Stoke FC
West Bromwich Albion	Wolverhampton Wanderers

The first official 'international' match between Scotland and England was played in Glasgow in 1872. It remains an important fixture for both countries to this day and was played annually until 1989. Nowadays they only play when competitions bring them together or when both management teams agree a friendly match would help with preparing for a major competition.

By the beginning of the 20th century, the need for a single body to oversee association football became apparent with the increasing popularity of international fixtures. The Football Association had chaired many discussions on setting up an international body but was deemed to be failing to make progress. So it fell to associations from seven other European countries, France, Belgium, Denmark, Netherlands, Spain, Sweden and Switzerland, to form an international association.

The *Fédération Internationale de Football Association* (FIFA) was founded in Paris on 21 May 1904. The French name and its acronym have remained to this day, even outside French-speaking countries. FIFA then adopted the Laws of the Game as laid down by the Football Association.

The growing popularity of the international game led to the admittance of FIFA representatives to the International Football Association Board in 1913, and the board now consists of four representatives from FIFA and one representative from each of the four British associations.

Historic games of football abound, but as we mentioned earlier, the games played on Christmas Day in 1914 stand out. This was when the German and British soldiers fighting in Flanders in Belgium agreed to call a truce for the day. Christmas carols were sung in English and German, and some of the troops played friendly games of football in no man's land between the trenches.

It was the centenary of this event during 2014, and Newark Town Football Club in the UK was awarded Lottery funds to finance an U-21s match against their German twin town of Emmendingen in remembrance of this day. There were many other similar games played, proving football's enduring ability to bring people together.

The Newark Town memorial match was played on August 24th, on the location in Ypres where one of these matches is believed to have taken place, according to letters sent home from the front in 1914 from a young Newark resident and a German soldier from Saxony, who both mentioned the games.

As we've already said, in addition to football being played by millions, both amateurs and professionals, even more people regularly go to football stadiums to follow their favourite teams, while billions watch the game on TV or streaming on the Internet. Over 265 million people from 210 countries regularly play football, and the game has the highest global television audience of any individual sport.

Football stadiums around the world are amazing structures, and the biggest can hold crowds of over 100,000. Wembley Stadium in London holds an unlikely record: It boasts the most toilets of any building in the world – a grand total of 2,618!

The increase in football's popularity over the last century has persuaded some nations to rename their organisations. Of the 45 national FIFA affiliates in which English is an official or primary language, almost all now use 'football' in their organisations' official names, with just Canada and the USA continuing to use the name 'soccer' in their titles.

Australia and New Zealand's association football governing bodies only changed their official names from soccer to football in 2007, with the New Zealanders saying this was because 'the international game is called football'. Samoa changed from Samoa Football (Soccer) Federation to Football Federation Samoa in 2009.

If you're living in North America, your young players are no doubt involved in youth soccer, and you'll find out all about this on the Internet. For those of you in the US, you could start with this link:

» www.usyouthsoccer.org/aboutus/FAQ

The history of the game has a real impact on how it's played today, and perhaps now that you've read and learned a little more about the development of the game, you will begin to understand the passions it invokes in its fervent supporters.

If you've read the entire book, you'll be able to hold your own in any conversation with the football fans among your family and friends and maybe even surprise them with a few facts about the game that they don't know. We certainly hope you'll enjoy football more, wherever you are watching, listening or even playing the game.

'It's a funny old game.'

(Jimmy Greaves)

Glossary

Added time
: Time allotted to compensate for breaks in the game caused by serious injuries or incidents on the pitch that halt play for any length of time. At amateur matches, the referees will just stop their stopwatch to compensate for these breaks in play. At professional levels, an official tracks the time, and the fourth official holds up a board at the end of each 45-minute period of play to indicate the added time to be played.

Advantage
: Play continuing after an infringement if the team gaining an advantage did not commit the offence. The referee indicates advantage is being played so all players are aware.

Assist
: A pass to a player that results in a goal being scored.

Back pass
: A pass from a player back to the goalkeeper or another member of his team, away from the direction of attack.

Ball
: The leather and rubber air-filled sphere on which the game is based. Players kick, head and chest the ball to each other and at the goal as part of the game.

Beach soccer
: A variation played on sand with pitches marked out on the sand.

Bench
: The seating area where substitutes, coaches and other members of the coaching staff sit during the match. At lower leagues, actual seating might not even exist, whereas at Premier League clubs, the seating area is usually covered to protect those using it from the worst of the weather.

Bicycle kick   A way of kicking the ball by leaping into the air, swinging the legs and scissor kicking the ball, usually behind the player. Frequently used in front of the goal.

Box (in the)   An alternative name for the penalty area.

Box to box   A midfielder is said to be a box-to-box player if he covers the whole length of the pitch, between the two penalty areas or boxes.

Calcio   Italian football game, rules first laid out in 1580.

Cambridge Rules   The original official laws of association football dating from 1848.

Chest(ing)   Moving the ball off the chest. Players frequently chest the ball down from a high kick.

Chip   A quick flick kick of the ball just above ground level, either over an opponent's legs or feet or to a player standing nearby.

Clearance kick   The long kick made by a goalkeeper or defender to clear the ball as far away from their own penalty area as possible. Taken from within the goal area or 6-yard box by the goalkeeper. Defenders also make clearance kicks.

Clean sheet   A goalie keeps a clean sheet when he doesn't allow any goals into his net during a match. The sheet in question being the scoring sheet used to record the match result.

Clinical   Adjective used in commentary to describe very precise ball movements or tackles or an overwhelming performance by one team over another.

Code(s)	Types of football played around the world and subject to differing laws. Variations include Association Football (Soccer), Rugby Union, Rugby League, American and Gaelic Football, Australian or Aussie Rules.
Coin toss	The way the referee decides which direction teams will play. He tosses a coin up in the air, and one of the team captains will choose heads or tails before it lands on the ground. The winner chooses which direction his team will attack in the first half of the game, and the other team gets to kick off. Teams swap ends for the second half. Sometimes just called the toss.
Corridor of uncertainty	A commentary description of the goal area of the pitch where balls can be challenged for by both sides equally. Usually used in relation to cross kicks and corner kicks.
Corner kick	If the ball goes behind the goal line after touching a defender (including the goalkeeper), the attacking team is awarded a corner kick.
Cross	A kick of the ball from the side of the pitch towards the centre or towards the goal. Wing backs are renowned for their ability to *cross* the ball to their strikers and assist in scoring goals. The ball is also said to cross the goal line when a goal is scored.
Cuju	Ancient ball game closely related to modern football played in China around 200 BC during the Han dynasty.
David Beckham territory	Pitch zone immediately outside the penalty area where David Beckham was considered to be most dangerous as a goal scorer.

Defender(s)/ Defence	Members of the team who halt attacks, tackling their opposition and taking the ball away from forwards and strikers. Some are also skilled at starting new attacks for their own team by taking the ball up the pitch before passing it on.
Derby/Local derby	A regular match between long-standing local rivals, teams such as Liverpool vs Everton, Manchester United vs Manchester City, Tottenham Hotspur vs Arsenal, Real Madrid vs Atlético Madrid.
Direct free kick	A free kick awarded by the referee which is allowed to be aimed straight into the goal.
Dribbling	The act of moving the ball along the ground with the feet – close control of the ball is required.
Drop ball	A ball dropped by the referee between two players to restart a match after an incident has halted play without obvious blame being apportioned to either team. Injuries, dogs invading pitches and even streakers can be responsible for drop-ball situations occurring.
Dubbin	Dubbing wax, a traditional way to waterproof leather football boots.
Each way	Term used to describe the fact that teams attack one goal in the first half of the match and the opposite goal in the second period. Typically 45 minutes each way, 15 minutes each way in extra time.
Engine room	A commentary term used to describe the defensive players' area from which new attacks will originate.
Extra time	30 minutes of additional play after the full-time whistle is blown when the scores are tied in a cup or competition match. 15 minutes are played each

way, and goals scored are added to the total score to produce a result. If, at the end of extra time the score remains tied, there is an option to move to a penalty shoot-out (see later).

Fair Play

A FIFA initiative designed to remove the less desirable elements from the game and ensure every game is played with good attitudes and without dissent from the players.

FIFA

Fédération Internationale de Football Association – the international governing body of the game since 1904.

Forward(s)

The members of the team who are responsible for attacking close to the goal, also known as *strikers*.

Foul

An infringement of the Laws that will result in the referee penalising the player and team.

Free kick(s)

Kicks awarded by the referee following an infringement of the Laws. Direct and indirect free kicks can be taken, as can corner kicks and goal kicks.

Freestyle

A version of football based on keeping the ball off the ground and doing acrobatic things with it.

Friendly

A match between club or international sides whose result will have no impact on tables. Used as a practice pre-season or before an important international match or competition to give coaches and players match experience without undue pressure on the result.

Futsal

Futebol de Salão is an indoor game played across South America, the Middle East and Africa, based in sports halls marked for basketball.

Goal	Either the structure through which goals must be scored to count or the act of scoring.
Goal Decision System	GDS, the Hawk-Eye-based system now used at senior level to confirm if the ball actually crosses the goal line.
Goal area	The marked zone immediately in front of the goal, also known as the 6-yard box. Special rules apply to indirect free kicks and drop balls in this zone.
Goalkeeper/ goalie/keeper	The only member of the team who is allowed to handle the ball on the pitch. Responsible for defending the goal against all attacks.
Goal kick	The clearance kick (normally taken by the goalkeeper) after the ball crosses the goal line directly after an attacking player touches it or if the ball goes into the goal directly from an indirect free kick. Always taken within the goal area or 6-yard box.
Goal line(s)	The lines at each end of the pitch on which the goal structures are placed. If the ball goes over these lines (outside the goal itself), depending on whether an attacker or defender last hit it, differing actions occur. Attack: a goal kick; defence: a corner kick.
Goalmouth scramble	No eggs are involved, just a melée of players trying to get to the ball, either to score or to defend and get it away from the goal.
Going nowhere	A commentary term used to describe a team passing the ball between themselves without advancing down the pitch.
Grassroots	The lowest level of competitive football; small clubs all around the world.

Grudge match	A regular fixture between rival teams that has resulted in clashes both on and off the pitch in the past. A return fixture against a team that won unfairly in a previous fixture.
Hacking	Originally part of the game; players could kick at their opponent's shins to make them give up the ball – banned with the division of the football codes in 1863.
Header(s)	The action of touching the ball with the head to divert it, either towards another player or at the goal.
High ball	Not a cocktail for footballers, but a ball kicked high in the air to get over defenders and reach the striker or other forwards. Frequently chested or headed down by the receiving player.
Indirect free kick	A kick awarded after an infringement but not allowed to go straight into the goal; it must first touch another player (from either side).
In the hole	A commentary term stolen from golf, used to describe an area of the pitch where strikers lurk (generally between midfield and the defensive line) in the hopes of picking up a pass and attacking the goal. In the hole is also used to describe a precise placement of a passing kick into the area just ahead of the striker(s).
Keepy-uppy	A part of freestyle football that involves keeping the ball off the ground for as long as possible.

Kemari	Japanese ball game played between the 10th and 16th centuries in Kyoto. A precursor to modern football.
Kick It Out	An FA programme designed to eliminate racism and all forms of discrimination throughout football.
La soule	French football game played in the 9th century.
Laws	The governing rules of the game which are designed to ensure the game is played fairly whenever and wherever it is played around the world.
Libero	The Italian term for a sweeper.
Mark(ing)	The act of tracking an opposition player to prevent them making an effective contribution. Marked players should find it difficult to play the ball without challenge. Marking is frequently qualified as being 'excellent' or 'poor' by journalists and commentators.
Midfield(er)	The central zone on the pitch; the players who attack and defend equally.
Net	The net is placed around the back of the goal posts to prevent balls going too far when kicked into the goal. Balls frequently hit the side netting from the wrong side when strikers are trying to score from wide positions.
No man's land	An area of the pitch where no players are currently playing. Defenders will sometimes kick a ball into this area to halt an attack, but teams will also use it as a zone for their fast running forwards to run towards and start an attack. Also the description of the land between trenches during the First World War where matches were played on 25 December 1914.

Off the ball	A description of an incident between players which takes place away from the main play around the ball. Players can also be moved off the ball when being tackled by the opposition.
Old firm derby	Specific to Glasgow, this is the fixture between longstanding city rivals Glasgow Rangers and Glasgow Celtic.
Officials	The team of between three and five people who ensure the game is played within the rules.
Offside	Once the simplest rule in the laws, now much too complicated, a player who is standing *offside* is not allowed to touch the ball or impede other players. If he does a free kick will be awarded, but standing in an offside position does not, in itself, result in a free kick – see the section on this in the book – it's far too complicated to explain in detail here.
Offside trap	Defenders will position themselves to attempt to trap the striker offside when the ball is kicked to him.
Olemac	Ancient ball courts used to play a ball game in Mesoamerica around 1200 BC.
On the road	Football clubs playing away games are described as being on the road. Winning while on the road, or winning away from home, is always thought to be more difficult than winning at a team's home ground where home support is believed to increase a home team's chances of winning.
Outfield	The main pitch excluding the penalty areas at either end.

Pass(ing)	The act of moving the ball from one player to another, generally along the ground, but sometimes through the air.
Pelé	Superstar Brazilian footballer born Edson Arantes do Nascimento in 1940. He played from the 1950s through to the 1970s. He retired in 1977 and is still acclaimed as the most successful footballer of all time.
Penalty (kick)	A free kick at goal awarded to an attacking team when a player is infringed inside the penalty area.
Penalty area	The 18-yard box marked out on the pitch in which an infringement by the defending team will result in the opposing team being awarded a penalty kick. Also the area in which the goalkeeper is allowed to handle the ball.
Penalty shoot-out	At the end of a cup competition match, if the result is still tied after extra time has been played, this is a short competitive period of play where five players from each side take turns to take penalty kicks at their opposition goalkeeper.
	If the result remains tied after all 10 have kicked the ball from the penalty spot, the competition moves to sudden death, and the first team to miss a goal while the opposition's next player scores will lose the match.
Penalty mark/spot	The small circle marked on the pitch inside the penalty area 12 yards (11 m) from the goal line, from which penalty kicks are taken. The ball is placed on the spot prior to kicking it at the goal.

Point blank | A kick at goal from close in is sometimes described as being at point-blank range – using gun terminology to describe the proximity to the goal when the shot is taken.

Postage stamp | A commentary explanation for the top back corner of the net; it's almost impossible for a goalie to defend against a shot aimed at this position. Strikers love landing the ball 'on a postage stamp'. Also, a description for a very small area of the pitch onto which a ball is precisely placed by a lobbed kick or pass.

Red card | The card shown to players who are being sent off the pitch for a second offence (following a previous yellow card offence) or for a sufficiently serious or dangerous offence that means instant dismissal from the game. The referee will record the offence in his notebook in case there is an appeal by the player after the match is over.

Respect | The FA's attempt to eliminate bad behaviour both on and off the pitch, for players and fans alike.

Row Z | The back row of the grandstand. Used in commentary to describe the location of massive clearance kicks by the defence which take the ball away from the attacking team by sending it 'out of the park'. Also used to describe badly miskicked strikes at goal.

Run out | Nothing to do with cricket (that's another of our guides) – coaches will give players 'a run out' by letting them play towards the end of a game once they believe the result is secure. Substitutes sitting shivering in the cold on the bench are always hoping for a run out if possible.

Save	The goalkeeper saves when he stops a goal from being scored. Defenders can also save goals from being scored.
Scissor kick	A way of kicking the ball by leaping into the air, swinging the legs to kick the ball, usually over the player's head. Frequently used in front of goal and also known as a bicycle kick.
Second half	The second section of a game, played for 45 minutes after the initial 45-minute first half.
Sepan tawak	A Malaysian ball game formalised in the 1750s.
Set piece plays	Planned and practiced moves associated with corner kicks or free kicks that provide the attacking team with the best chance of scoring.
Shin pads	Protective foam pads worn inside socks to protect the shins and ankles.
Shoot/Shot	The action of kicking the ball hard at the goal to score.
Shoulder charge	An illegal move that will be penalised by the referee. Players are allowed to jostle each other gently, but not charge at other players or shove them off the ball.
Sidelines	The long sides of the pitch, also known as touchlines.
6-yard box	The alternative name for the goal area, the oblong marked area on the pitch immediately in front of the goal posts from which the goalkeeper will take goal kicks.
Soccer	The alternative name for football based on a contraction of the full title Association Football, Assoc = soccer.

Spot kick

An alternative term for a penalty kick taken from the penalty spot.

Stoppages

Halts in play during a game that are tracked and timed by the officials to calculate additional time that will be added on at the end of each half.

Street football

A style of football used across the poorer nations of the world. It's a city game with no offside rule and either clothing as goalposts or a goalmouth marked in chalk on a wall. Teams can be differing numbers and with no officials the rules are often invented on the spot as the game progresses.

Striker(s)

Nothing to do with stopping work. This is an attacking player or players, frequently found standing in or around the penalty area.

Strip

A set of football kit in club or team colours: shirt, shorts and socks and sometimes a track suit.

Substitute(s)

Subs, or substitutes, are players in addition to the starting 11 who are allowed to replace players on the pitch in the case of injury or at senior level, at the choice of the manager. They sit on the *bench* while waiting their turn to play.

Sudden death

This is the final section of a penalty shoot-out competition. If the score remains tied after all 10 players (5 from each side) have taken their penalties, then players take spot kicks until one team fails to score and the other succeeds.

Sweeper

A roving player, based in the centre of the defence, who can create attacks as well as halt them.

The channel

Not the strip of sea between the UK and France, but a commentary description, as in: down the channel, in the channel. Used to describe the ball being passed parallel to the side of the pitch. See our commentary diagram on page 15.

Throw-in(s)	The act of throwing the ball back onto the pitch after it has crossed the sideline.
Toss	The start of the game when the referee throws a coin in the air and asks one team captain to call heads or tails to decide which end of the pitch his team will attack. See also *coin toss*.
Unmarked	A player who has managed to evade the opposition to find space on the pitch to receive the ball is deemed unmarked. This can either be an example of poor marking or of a very clever attacking player.
Wall	A formation of defensive players designed to protect the goal against a free kick.
Wing(s)/Wing back(s)	The players who play closest to the touch or sidelines. Usually they are fast sprinters with good ball crossing skills. The left wing back is often a left-footed player.
Yellow card	Warning card shown to players who infringe the Laws to warn them not to repeat similar offences or they will be shown a second yellow card, immediately followed by a red card, which results in them being sent off the pitch. The yellow-card warning is recorded in the referee's notebook.

Weblinks

>> www.sueportersguide.com

Our own website, with lots of useful information including clickable links for you to access all the links in our books.

Football governance and general information

>> www.fifa.com

>> www.thefa.com

The Laws

>> www.fifa.com/aboutfifa/officialdocuments/doclists/laws.html

>> www.thefa.com/football-rules-governance/laws/football-11-11/law-1---the-field-of-play

Fan information and how to play

>> www.worldsoccer.about.com

>> www.bbc.co.uk/sport/0/football

>> news.bbc.co.uk/sport1/hi/football/skills/default.stm

>> en.wikipedia.org/wiki/Freestyle_football#Red_Bull_Street_Style_Kuwait_.28_KWT_RBSS_.29_2012

>> www.freestylefootball.org/world_tour/general

>> www.usyouthsoccer.org/aboutus/FAQ

World Cup

>> http://www.fifa.com/worldcup

Official explanations of the offside law

>> http://www.fifa.com/mm/document/footballdevelopment/ refereeing/02/36/01/11/27_06_2014_new--lawsofthegameweben_ neutral.pdf (see from page 108 of this pdf booklet)

>> www.thefa.com/football-rules-governance/laws/football-11-11/law- 11---offside.aspx

Fantasy football

>> fantasy.premierleague.com

Football fan information

>> www.footballfans.eu

>> www.footballfancast.com

>> www.kickitout.org/about

Football team strips

>> www.worldsoccershop.com

>> www.rebelsport.com.au

>> www.soccer.com

Other kit suppliers

>> www.discountfootballkits.com

>> www.prosocceruk.co.uk

>> www.bluemoonsport.co.uk

>> www.sportingtouch.com

IF YOU'VE ENJOYED THIS BOOK, WHY NOT LOOK OUT FOR OUR OTHER GUIDES:

RUGBY MADE SIMPLE (Published Sept 2015)

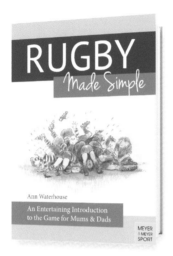

PLANNED PUBLICATION:

CRICKET MADE SIMPLE (Due out in April 2016)

Check our website: www.sueportersguide.com for more links and information on all these games.

Credits

Text:	© Copyright 2015 Ann M Waterhouse
Illustrations:	© Copyright 2015 Amanda Stiby Harris
Cover Illustration:	© Copyright 2015 Amanda Stiby Harris
Copyediting:	Elizabeth Evans
Layout, Typesetting, Jacket & Cover:	Eva Feldmann
Illustration page 41:	© stihii/shutterstock.com

Notes